Exploring Context in Information Behavior

Seeker, Situation, Surroundings, and Shared Identities

Synthesis Lectures on Information Concepts, Retrieval, and Services

Editor

Gary Marchionini, *University of North Carolina, Chapel Hill*

Synthesis Lectures on Information Concepts, Retrieval, and Services publishes short books on topics pertaining to information science and applications of technology to information discovery, production, distribution, and management. Potential topics include: data models, indexing theory and algorithms, classification, information architecture, information economics, privacy and identity, scholarly communication, bibliometrics and webometrics, personal information management, human information behavior, digital libraries, archives and preservation, cultural informatics, information retrieval evaluation, data fusion, relevance feedback, recommendation systems, question answering, natural language processing for retrieval, text summarization, multimedia retrieval, multilingual retrieval, and exploratory search.

Exploring Context in Information Behavior: Seeker, Situation, Surroundings, and Shared Identities
Naresh Kumar Agarwal

ISBN: 978-3-031-01185-6   paperback
ISBN: 978-3-031-02313-2   ebook
ISBN: 978-3-031-00220-5   hardcover

DOI 10.1007/978-3-031-02313-2

A Publication in the Springer series
SYNTHESIS LECTURES ON INFORMATION CONCEPTS, RETRIEVAL, AND SERVICES, #61
Series Editor: Gary Marchionini, University of North Carolina, Chapel Hill

Series ISSN: 1947-945X Print   1947-9468 Electronic

Cover concept and watercolor painting by Naresh Kumar Agarwal.

Exploring Context in Information Behavior

Seeker, Situation, Surroundings, and Shared Identities

Naresh Kumar Agarwal
Simmons School of Library & Information Science

SYNTHESIS LECTURES ON INFORMATION CONCEPTS, RETRIEVAL, AND SERVICES #61

ABSTRACT

The field of human information behavior runs the gamut of processes from the realization of a need or gap in understanding, to the search for information from one or more sources to fill that gap, to the use of that information to complete a task at hand or to satisfy a curiosity, as well as other behaviors such as avoiding information or finding information serendipitously. Designers of mechanisms, tools, and computer-based systems to facilitate this seeking and search process often lack a full knowledge of the context surrounding the search. This context may vary depending on the job or role of the person; individual characteristics such as personality, domain knowledge, age, gender, perception of self, etc.; the task at hand; the source and the channel and their degree of accessibility and usability; and the relationship that the seeker shares with the source. Yet researchers have yet to agree on what context really means. While there have been various research studies incorporating context, and biennial conferences on context in information behavior, there lacks a clear definition of what context is, what its boundaries are, and what elements and variables comprise context.

In this book, we look at the many definitions of and the theoretical and empirical studies on context, and I attempt to map the conceptual space of context in information behavior. I propose theoretical frameworks to map the boundaries, elements, and variables of context. I then discuss how to incorporate these frameworks and variables in the design of research studies on context. We then arrive at a unified definition of context. This book should provide designers of search systems a better understanding of context as they seek to meet the needs and demands of information seekers. It will be an important resource for researchers in Library and Information Science, especially doctoral students looking for one resource that covers an exhaustive range of the most current literature related to context, the best selection of classics, and a synthesis of these into theoretical frameworks and a unified definition. The book should help to move forward research in the field by clarifying the elements, variables, and views that are pertinent. In particular, the list of elements to be considered, and the variables associated with each element will be extremely useful to researchers wanting to include the influences of context in their studies.

KEYWORDS

information behavior, information seeking, context, situation, environment, task, user, source, contextual identity framework

To Sikkim—the land that nurtured me
My family and friends—you are my anchor
And to all those who paved the path for me to walk on

Contents

Figures

Tables

Preface

When I was pursuing my Ph.D. in Information Systems at the National University of Singapore in 2008, I would have frequent meetings with my co-advisor Yunjie (Calvin) Xu. As we worked on designing a research framework for a survey study of knowledge workers in Singapore, he suggested it might be a good idea to review the literature on context. At the time, I didn't know what I was getting into.

When you ask a question to someone, and you don't get an easy "yes" or "no" answer, and the person says, "It depends," that is when you know that the person is talking about context. In my month-long investigation following the meeting with my co-advisor, I realized that understanding context was not very different from peeling onions. The more I thought I understood, the more I uncovered new layers that provided more questions than answers. Was context something which contains, i.e., the environment that surrounds a seeker of information? Was it the seeker as the person, or the information source that the person looked to for information? Was it the channel of communication that the seeker used to reach the source? Or was it the factors that impacted the choice of the source? Was it the task at hand, or simple everyday curiosity? Was it place and time? Was it situation? Or was it a shared identity or kinship with a team or group one was a part of? As Dervin (1997) wrote, "the very question [of what is context] turns out to be almost embarrassing, and certainly a question leading to a quest that demands extraordinary tolerance of chaos" (p.13).

It took me many months to wrap my head around what context in information behavior might mean. Context has been an important part of the empirical and theoretical studies that I have conducted in the years since then. Whether I am looking at medical residents in a hospital, the interactions of a child with an iPad, the information-seeking behavior of students, the information practices of faculty members, or theoretical and conceptual studies synthesizing different phenomena, an understanding of context plays an important role in the design of those studies.

I developed theoretical frameworks to understand the different aspects of context, what its boundaries and elements are, and how context can be applied in the design of research studies. This book is an endeavor to synthesize and conceptualize the research and understandings of context in the information behavior literature so far, and my own prior research, and to arrive at a definition of context in information behavior. The proposed frameworks should help future researchers as well as search system designers. Now that I've shared with you my context for writing this book, we are ready, quoting Dervin (1997), "to demonstrate extraordinary tolerance for chaos, and to talk about context!" ☺

Naresh Agarwal

Acknowledgments

As I seek to thank people who were by my side as I wrote this book, I think it might be useful to situate these within the contextual factors of task or situation, the surroundings or environment, the information need, the actor or seeker, the source or system, the actor-source relationship, and time/space.

The task or situation was that I was applying for a 6-month sabbatical from the Simmons School of Library and Information Science (SLIS) (the *environment*). The *need* then was a worthy project to work on during the sabbatical. I am thankful to Professor Gary Marchionini and the reviewers for approving my proposal. My heartfelt thanks to my wonderful Dean Eileen Abels, the review committee and the Provost for approving my sabbatical, which enabled me to work on this project. I'm grateful for the support of all my colleagues at SLIS.

I was the *actor* or *seeker* in need of information through the process of synthesizing and writing. The various information *sources* were the proceedings of the information seeking in context conferences, information behavior books, and primarily, my own prior research on context since my Ph.D. days at the National University of Singapore. I'm grateful to my graduate student assistant, Alison Fisher, who worked closely with me in helping gather literature, making suggestions and meeting with me online as I worked on the book. My familiarity with the sources and the literature (*actor-source relationship*) was very useful in putting the book together.

The *time* was the November 2016–August 2017 period when I worked on the book, as well as later period of reviews and revisions (September–October, 2017) until publication. I'm grateful to Diane Cerra for being so supportive throughout and helping secure the approval for letting me design my own self-painted cover. My sincere thanks to the reviewers Professors Sanda Erdelez and Barbara Wildemuth for their very thorough review and comments. I believe that addressing all their comments greatly helped to improve the book. The *place* where I worked was my home office in Sharon, Massachusetts, typing away on my Windows laptop. I'm eternally grateful for the unconditional love and support of my wife Dr. Archana Agarwal and the joy of my two kids—9-year old Eesha and 2 ½-year old Ishaan.

I'm thankful to my family in India who have been with me throughout. Last, but not the least, I'm indebted to my friends ('sāthī' in Nepali or Hindi, or "priya snehitaḥ" or "mitraṃ" in Sanskrit), who have always been there for me—whether in person, over the phone, or through social media.

Naresh Agarwal
October 14, 2017

CHAPTER 1

Introduction: Why Context?

Imagine that you are a typical information seeker (if there is such a person), and that you have just encountered a need for information. It could be in an everyday life situation at home—like booking an air ticket, buying new shoes, or deciding on a college—or at a work or study task, like working on a project or assignment. You will likely then choose to start looking for information to fulfill your need. Your search for information may be from people—friends or colleagues or a reference librarian (either face-to-face, using asynchronous communication such as email, or synchronous communication such as phone or instant messaging), from physical books or manuals, or from online websites and search interfaces such as Google or Wikipedia (Agarwal, 2011; Agarwal, Xu, and Poo, 2011). You may go online first (Agarwal, Xu, and Poo, 2011) (on a smartphone or computer), using an app or a browser, to a search engine such as Google or a site such as Wikipedia, social media such as Facebook or Twitter, or ask Siri, Cortana, or Alexa. You might decide to email or to text a friend or colleague using SMS, iMessage, WhatsApp, Facebook Messenger, SnapChat, Allo, etc. so as to reach out without completely interrupting what your friend or colleague (the source) might be doing at the moment. You might call this source using your phone, on WhatsApp, Messenger, Skype, or Facetime Audio, or speak to the person over video—using Facetime, Google Hangout, Skype, or GoToMeeting. Finally, and increasingly often as a last resort (sometimes even when the person is within geographical proximity or in the same room—see the discussion at CollegeNet, 2015), you might reach out to the person face-to-face. You might even decide to seek information collaboratively as a pair with a teammate, as a team or a group, or reach out to a community of people for answers—on Facebook, Twitter, or other online communities like blogs, Quora.com, Yahoo Answers, etc. As you can see, your choice of action, and the source or channel to use will be based on specific contextual factors.

In order for a reference librarian or a search engine to adequately understand and help an information seeker, it would be helpful to understand the context/situation of the information need that got the person searching in the first place (except in cases where both the question and answer are factual and relatively straightforward). A depersonalized search engine doesn't always get the right results; for example, a search for "apple" on Google may give results related to the Apple computer and other products by the company. Yet it might be that the person searching is a farmer or someone looking for apple picking. While this could be resolved by incorporating some of the context in the query formulation, there are other aspects of a person's context, like expertise and stage of the project at hand, that may be difficult to include in a query. This simple example of the search for apple describes linguistic ambiguity. In real-life situations and work-based tasks such as planning travel, buying something, adopting a pet, working on a team project, or conducting research, which are often more complex, it would help if the search engine knew more about the person's task or situation. This knowledge about the task, situation, person, etc. is something that can be described as the knowledge about the person's context when looking for information. As Fatemi (2015) posits, "the Internet will soon be about context and discovery, increasing its focus on serving up content consumers don't know they need yet."

"Context is the quark of communication theory; everyone knows it is there, but nobody is sure where—or what—it is. In the last thirty years or so, virtually everyone writing about communication theory 'discovers' that what is really needed is a theory of context" (Keith, 1994, p. 229). This notion of context has received increased attention in information science conferences and publications over the last two decades, along with related terms such as situation, setting, and environment. Numerous authors have argued for information retrieval research to incorporate more context (Cool, 2001; Järvelin and Ingwersen, 2004; Ingwersen and Järvelin, 2005; Beaulieu, 2006; Ruthven, 2008; Fidel, 2012). As Dervin wrote (1997), "The good news is that context is hot. Everywhere one turns in literatures of the social sciences and humanities focusing on how humans make sense of their worlds one sees increasing references to context" (p. 13). Cool (2001) attributed this increased attention to the thinking that "in order to better understand information-seeking behavior and information retrieval interaction, greater attention needs to be directed to the information spaces within which these activities are embedded" (p. 5). The purpose of the first Information Interaction in Context (IIiX) conference in 2006 was "to investigate how the concept of context can be understood and exploited to make information systems truly interactive" (Ruthven et al., 2006, p. i). Context continues to be "hot" 20 years later, with the term becoming increasingly important in fields such as information science, information retrieval, information interaction and human-computer interaction (Fidel, 2012). Conferences such as Information Seeking in Context (ISIC) and IIiX have continually discussed it. In 2016, the first CHIIR (ACM SIGIR Conference on Human Information Interaction and Retrieval) conference was held, representing the merger of IIiX and the Human Computer Information Retrieval symposium (HCIR).

Lee (2011) writes that context is inherently relational: it is always context of, about, or surrounding something or someone. Lee also cites a number of past definitions and descriptions of context. As the title of this book suggests, we are interested in the context of, about or surrounding the actor engaged in information behavior. Before we start looking in-depth at context, we will briefly summarize the field of information behavior research as a whole and discuss the importance of context within it.

1.1   THE FIELD OF INFORMATION BEHAVIOR

Information behavior is a field of research encompassing a wide range of essential human activities, including "accidental encountering of, needing, finding, choosing, using, and sometimes even avoiding, information" (Case and Given, 2016, p. 4). It is concerned with information use and nonuse, the processing of found information, and reasons for unsuccessful processing (Ford, 2015). Several key concepts and sub-areas within information behavior are defined in Table 1.1 below. The definitions for actor, information need, and information seeking are adapted from Agarwal (2015).

Table 1.1: Definition of terms related to information behavior	
Actor	Seeker/user/person who is looking for information or who finds information unexpectedly. According to Dervin's sense-making methodology, this actor is a "body-mind-heart-spirit moving through time and space, with a past history, present reality and future dreams or ambitions" (Foreman-Wernet, 2003, p. 7; Agarwal, 2012).
Information Need	The recognition that your knowledge is inadequate to satisfy a goal (Case and Given, 2016). Line (1974) distinguishes need from other related terms such as *want*, *demand*, and *requirement* (also see Agarwal, 2015). Taylor (1968) defines information need as one of four types: visceral, conscious, formalized, and compromised, depending upon the degree of clarity and articulation of the need. Wilson (1981, p. 8) suggests avoiding the term *information need* and instead referring to "information-seeking toward the satisfaction of needs." Savolainen (2012) examined the various ways of studying the triggers for information need, and deduced that there were three different ways that people understood information need to happen—as part of a situation, as arising in a work task, or happening during a discourse or part of a conversation. These contexts for need are not mutually exclusive and could co-occur.
Information Seeking	A conscious effort to acquire information in response to a gap in our knowledge (Case and Given, 2016). Bates (2002) characterizes information seeking as either *active* or *passive* and either *directed* or *undirected*.
Information Searching	"A subset of information seeking, particularly concerned with the interactions between information user…and computer-based information systems" (Wilson, 1999, p. 263). An *information retrieval* system leads the user to documents that help satisfy information need (Robertson, 1981) or solve problems (Belkin, 1984).

Information Use	"What information does to or for the recipient and for his or her problem or situation" (Taylor, 1991, p. 221). Wilson (2000, p. 50) defined information use as "the physical and mental acts involved in incorporating the information found into the person's existing information base." "It may involve...physical acts such as marking sections in a text... [or] mental acts..[such as comparing]...new information with existing knowledge" (Wilson, 2000, p. 50). Savolainen (2009) drew from approaches in organization science (the notions of *epistemic work* suggested by Cook and Brown (1999) and *knowing in practice* proposed by Orlikowski (2002)) to conceptualize information use as a process that is contextualized in action or practice. Epistemic work conceptualizes information use as the employment of tacit and explicit knowledge in the service of knowing, where knowing is understood as an inherent part of action. Knowing in practice sees information use as construction and reconstruction of knowledgeability in and through action (Savolainen, 2009). Specific examples of reading and learning as information use include Renear and Palmer (2009), Zhang et al., (2011), Latham (2014), and Vakkari (2016).
Information Encountering/ Serendipity	In Agarwal (2015), I define serendipity in information behavior as "an incident-based, unexpected discovery of information leading to an *aha!* moment when a naturally alert actor is in a passive, non-purposive state or in an active, purposive state, followed by a period of incubation leading to insight and value." At the panel *Research Perspectives on Serendipity and Information Encountering* at the ASIS&T 2016 Annual Meeting, there was a suggestion to build consensus on using the term *information encountering* to denote serendipity in information behavior (Erdelez et al., 2016). Also see Erdelez' (1997) conceptualization of encountering and Makri and Blandford's work on serendipity (Makri and Blandford, 2012; Makri et al., 2014).

Information Avoiding	The tendency of people to "avoid, ignore, or deny information," especially "if paying attention to it will cause mental discomfort or dissonance" (Case et al., 2005, p. 354). Wilson (1995) points out that filtering or "nonuse" behavior can be both efficient and rational if it is a matter of conscious policy when "presented with more information than one could absorb" (p. 45). If entire groups of people do not get the same information as other groups (I would assert this would apply to individuals who tend to avoid information as well), we speak of them as having a "knowledge gap" or being "information poor" (Case and Given, 2016, p. 119).

Early research on information seeking was chiefly system-centered (Vakkari, 1999), focusing on information sources, library use, and the performance of retrieval systems (Case and Given, 2016). In the 1970s, the focus of research in information science moved away from information systems toward the person as a searcher, creator, and user of information (Ellis, 2011). This user-centered paradigm has sought to understand both the commonalities and the differences in the ways people interact with information in the world around them.

Pettigrew, Fidel, and Bruce (2001) classify major conceptual developments in the user-centered information behavior literature into three categories: cognitive, social and multifaceted. Cognitive approaches cover models and theories focusing fundamentally on individual user attributes and knowledge structures (Belkin, 1990). Social approaches focus on the way an individual's interaction with information is shaped by social norms, networks, and organizations (Talja, Tuominen, and Savolainen, 2005). The area of "information practice" (Savolainen, 2007, 2008), as distinct from information behavior follows this social approach. We will discuss information practices briefly in Section 2.2.3, under the sub-section "Other information behavior and practices affected by context." Multifaceted approaches cover the cognitive, social, and organizational context (see Ingwersen and Järvelin, 2005).

The cognitive viewpoint has been the dominant approach in most user-centered models (Wilson, 1981; Krikelas, 1983; Ellis, 1989; Kuhlthau, 1991; etc.) and some system-centered models (e.g., Belkin, 1990; Ingwersen, 1992; Saracevic, 1996; Spink, 1997; Järvelin and Ingwersen, 2004; Ingwersen and Järvelin, 2005; Järvelin, 2007). More naturalistic and interpretive studies (e.g., Chatman, 1996; Solomon, 1999; McKenzie, 2003) have used social approaches. These are less common in empirical work than the cognitive viewpoint. Apart from the cognitive and social approaches, there are affective approaches that study the role of emotion in information behavior (Kuhlthau, 1991; Nahl and Bilal, 2007; Savolainen, 2014). Dervin (Dervin, 1992; Dervin and Foreman-Wernet, 2012; Agarwal, 2012), Leckie et al. (1996), Johnson (1997), Kari and Savolainen (2003), Byström and Hansen (2005), Karunakaran, Reddy, and Spence (2013), and others have proposed multifaceted models that bring together both cognitive and social approaches. These multifaceted approaches emphasize the importance of social, organizational, and situational factors on an individual's cognitive state.

1.1.1   WHY IS CONTEXT RELEVANT TO INFORMATION BEHAVIOR?

If we did not take context into consideration, then it would be reasonable to assume that information behavior follows a predictable pattern, i.e., people look for information in a certain way all the time (for example, perhaps they always choose information sources based on their quality or accessibility). The danger of such assumptions is that they paint everyone and every behavior with a broad brush, without investigating the nuances of the conditions under which these behaviors might differ. People don't behave the same way all the time. Every situation is unique, involving different people, different surroundings, and a different series of events. Our behavior is affected by factors outside our control. That is why context becomes important.

As Jansen and Rieh (2010) wrote, "information is difficult, if not impossible, to define separately from a given context" (p. 1522). Context is a key part of any study of any aspect of information behavior—be it information seeking, information encountering, information avoiding, information use, collaborative information seeking, mobile information behavior, etc. Each of these will vary according to the actor and his/her social context, the source or system, the workplace or everyday life, and the relationships and the interactions between these. Identifying and understanding those factors then becomes a primary imperative in investigating research questions in any of these areas of information behavior.

While earlier system-centered research investigated the contextual variables of users in certain contexts, later user-centered research focused first on the person, regardless of context (Fidel, 2012). In the first ISIC conference in 1996, the notion of "in-context" research was formally established (Fidel, 2012), with researchers such as Wilson (1997) incorporating the "person-in-context" into their information seeking models. Other early models emphasizing context include Byström and Järvelin (1995) and Savolainen (1995).

In the last few decades, "context-awareness" or "context-aware computing" has become increasingly important in the design of software systems. Context-awareness is defined as "the use of context to provide task-relevant information and/or services to the user" (Dey and Abowd, 1999, p. 1). Traxler (2011) mentions the shifting role of context in the mobile-connected world, where the actor is driving system design for personal mobile digital technologies (as the person could carry the mobile anywhere), as opposed to an organization, school or library where the actor might have earlier gone to use computers. "We now cross from a technical or reformist account of context to a radical or social account and a shift of context-aware mobile learning from a component of mobile learning to the educational component of context-aware services and experiences" (Traxler, 2011, p. 6). This has implications for mobile learning, for the relationship between learners and their educational institutions, and on work, jobs, businesses, and the economy; on perceptions of time, space and place; on the individual, their identity and the nature of communities; on knowledge, knowing, understanding and learning and consequently on a changed meaning for "context" and its role (Traxler, 2011). Traxler and Kukulska-Hulme (2016) further discuss technologies and applications for context-aware mobile learning in various settings.

1.2   WHAT IS CONTEXT?

"To ask a question [what is context?] that is so little asked may prove useful…after an extended effort to review treatments of context, the only possible conclusion is that there is no term that is more often used, less often defined, and when defined defined so variously as context" (Dervin, 1997, pp. 13-14). While researchers have made various attempts to define context—resulting in terms such as environment, container, situation, etc.—there isn't a single accepted definition of context as yet. Most literature in the field fails to address the problem of context theoretically (Dervin, 1997; Johnson, 2003; Lueg, 2002; Courtright, 2007; Agarwal, Xu, and Poo, 2009).

An inherent problem with defining context is that it is emergent, continually renegotiated and defined in the course of action (Kuutti, 1999; Dourish, 2004; Allen, Karanasios, and Slavova, 2011). "'Context' is a slippery notion. Perhaps appropriately, it is a concept that keeps to the periphery, and slips away when one attempts to define it" (Dourish, 2004, p. 29).

Dervin (1997, pp. 14-15) lists three conceptualizations of context in the literature. She argues that for many, "context has the potential of being virtually anything that is not defined as the phenomenon of interest…a kind of container in which the phenomenon resides." Similarly, Lee (2011) describes "everything else" as the broadest formulation of context, i.e., everything in the universe that is not the actor. Dervin says that a second group struggles with trying to determine which of an "inexhaustible list of factors" will be included in context. For a third group of researchers, context is "the carrier of meaning…an inextricable surround without which any possible understanding of human behavior becomes impossible".

Lee (2011, p. 97) classifies the literature and formulations on context as one of three types—$Context_1$, $Context_2$, and $Context_3$. $Context_1$ is the set of symbolic expressions or representations that surround the actor and helps one to express, make sense of, translate or otherwise act upon or within the actor. This relates to the idea of "where I stand" (Lee, 2011) or situatedness (Lindblom and Ziemke, 2003) of the actor within an environment where the actor's thinking and behavior is informed and dictated by the environment. $Context_2$ is the objective or socially constructed characteristics and conditions of the situation in which the actor is, appears or occurs. Examples include: location; temperature; being under water; position within the reporting structure of an organizational hierarchy; existence and accessibility of other surrounding people or objects (Lee, 2011). Lee describes $Context_3$ as aspects of the mental or physical state, disposition, intentions, identity, habits or recent experiences of the actor that bear upon how the actor interprets, understands, acts within, or what the actor notices of, the situation at hand. Context$_3$ can take the form of the actor's own state/disposition or the state/disposition of other people that are relevant to the task/matter at hand (e.g., co-workers in a team, or collaborators).

We can understand Context$_1$ as the environment, Context$_2$ as the situation at a particular time and space, and Context$_3$ as the actor's personal and social characteristics. Lee writes that a great deal of human communication takes place at the intersection between these three types of context. In the section below, we discuss the many definitions and types of context. I arrive at my own unified definition in Chapter 5.

1.2.1   THE MANY FACETS AND TYPES OF CONTEXT

Researchers have used many terms to describe context or its facets, some of them similar in meaning, but not always equivalent. This points to their differing perceptions of context. The source of this disagreement is no doubt the vast complexity of the topic; individual studies have focused on such a variety of contextual factors—e.g., the actor, the work role or life role, the situation, the source or system, and interactions among these—that it is very difficult to arrive at a definition that adequately accounts for all such factors.

Dourish (2004) makes a distinction between the objective/positivist and subjective/phenomenological view. "Positivist theories seek objective, independent descriptions of social phenomena, abstracting from the detail of particular occasions or settings, often in favor of broad statistical trends and idealised models." (Dourish, 2004, p. 20). "Phenomenological theories are subjective and qualitative in orientation"; "social facts are emergent properties of interactions, not pre-given or absolute but negotiated, contested, and subject to continual processes of interpretation and re-interpretation"; "…abstract categories… are things that need to be imposed on the world through our interactions with it and with each other, rather than things that exist within it" (Dourish, 2004, p. 21). These views held by researchers also influence the way they understand and categorize context. Researchers might identity themselves more with a "positivist" orientation using scientific, quantitative reasoning and approaches in their research methods, or more with an "interpretivist" orientation using humanistic, qualitative approaches in their research. They might also adopt other stances such as "critical," or straddle across these different orientations and approaches using mixed-methods.

We discuss the sometimes-competing terms below. I arrived at these various types through a review of the literature on context, and my own prior work in the area. The initial categories such as context as environment, setting, etc., were especially informed by Courtright (2007), Agarwal (2009a), and Agarwal, Xu, and Poo (2009). The list grew as more literature was reviewed, and various ways of labeling and categorizing context were identified.

a. Context as Environment or Container

In many studies of a person's information seeking or information retrieval behavior, context has been understood as an environment or container surrounding the person (for example, Rieh, 2004; Lamb, King, and Kling, 2003)—aspects of a person's life or work role that would influence why a person is looking for information, and the degree to which he/she/they would be satisfied with a particular answer. Other research that sees context as environment includes, for example, Janes and Silverstein (2003) and Taylor (1991). Lee (2011) defines context as a "set of things, factors, elements and attributes that are related to a target entity in important ways (e.g., operationally, semantically, conceptually or pragmatically) but are not so closely related to the target entity that they are considered to be exclusively part of the target entity itself" (p. 96). Context as environment would fall under Dourish's (2004) description of the positivist view of context; see Figure 1.1.

Figure 1.1: Context as environment or container.

b. Context as Setting

This is similar to the environment/container viewpoint. Research using this term includes, for example, Byström (1997), Pettigrew (2000), Davies and McKenzie (2004), McKenzie (2004) and Brown (2010). Allen and Kim (2000) view contexts as the socially defined settings in which information users are found, e.g., a work setting such as an office or a factory. Most studies in libraries, archives, and museums treat context as a setting, where different aspects of user needs and behavior are studied. Here, the setting is typically described as a type of library (public libraries, academic libraries, special libraries like corporate, medical, law, church, or prison libraries, etc.), and particular archives or museums. Several journals in Library and Information Science demonstrate this emphasis on context as setting. Examples include the *Journal of Academic Librarianship, Journal of the Medical Library Association, Journal of Business and Finance Librarianship, Law Library Journal, Science and Technology Libraries, Archival Science*, etc. Context as setting would also fall under Dourish's (2004) positivist view of context.

Figure 1.2: **Context as setting.**

c. Context as Role

Other research subsumes specific aspects of the environment, surrounding, container, setting with aspects of the actor to focus on the service or work role as context. This is evidenced by journals dedicated to specific work within settings. For example, in a library setting, this work role context is seen in the journal titles *Reference and User Services Quarterly*, *Reference Librarian*, *Music Reference Services Quarterly*, *Collection Management*, *Technical Services Quarterly*, *Library Collections, Acquisition and Technical Services*, and more general types of work in journals such as *Information Processing and Management*. Context is also studied for other work roles, such as doctors (Gorman, 1999; Grad et al., 2011), lawyers (Sutton, 1994; Cole and Kuhlthau, 2000), managers (Choo and Auster, 1993; Edwards et al., 2013), etc. Studies have also looked at everyday life roles of the actor, such as citizen or voter, consumer, hobbyist, gatekeeper, patient, student, and so on (Abrahamson et al., 2008; Case, 2010; Cole, 2013; Yates and Partridge, 2015, among many others). Leckie and Pettigrew (1997) discuss information behavior in light of role theory, which originated in psychology and sociology.

Figure 1.3: **Context as role** (physician, graduate, and cyclist).

d. Context as Situation

A situation is "a set of related activities, or a set of related stories, that occur over time" (Sonnenwald, 1999, p. 180). People have used the term *situation* interchangeably with *context* (e.g., Allen, 1997), but some researchers have sought to disambiguate the two. Sonnenwald (1999) states that context is larger than a situation and may consist of a variety of situations. "Different contexts may have different possible types of situations" (p. 180). Cool (2001) extends Sonnenwald's notion to suggest that "contexts are frameworks of meaning, and situations are the dynamic environments within which interpretive processes unfold, become ratified, change, and solidify" (p. 8). Likewise, for Allen and Kim (2000), "within each of these broad contexts, different situations occur…individuals may be situated in different ways in the context" (p. 1). McCreadie and Rice (1999, p. 58) define context as the "larger picture in which the potential user operates; the larger picture in which the information system is developed and operates, and potential information exists," and situation as "the particular set of circumstances from which a need for information arises." Courtright (2007) sees context as including those elements that have a more lasting and predictable influence on information [behavior] than situation (closer to life world and information world, discussed below), whereas situation is seen as a potential part of context. A situation can also be considered something that "happens" to people, where actors deal with things not because they want to, but because they have to. German philosopher Martin Heidegger describes this as "thrownness" (Dahlstrom, 2013). "The thrower of the project is thrown in his own throw. How can we account for this freedom? We cannot. It is simply a fact, not caused or grounded, but the condition of all causation and grounding" (Inwood, 1999). A close parallel is the idea of situatedness, where the actor's behavior and cognitive processes are believed primarily to be the outcome of a close coupling between the actor and the environment (Lindblom and Ziemke, 2003).

e. Context as the Actor's Mind

Some researchers see context as arising in the mind of the actor. Here, context becomes internal, and includes cognitive-affective factors. Wilson (1999) talks about the actor's experience of cognitive dissonance affecting information need (pp. 256-257). Lee (2011) describes it as one of three formulations of context in the literature—"aspects of the mental or physical state, disposition, intentions, identity or recent experiences of an actor that bear upon how she interprets, understands, acts within, or what she notices of, the situation at hand" (p. 97). This would fall under Dervin (1997)'s description of context, and Dourish (2004)'s characterization of the phenomenological approach to understanding context.

Figure 1.4: Context as the actor's mind.

f. Context as Information Horizon, Field, and Pathways

"Within a context and situation is an 'information horizon' in which we can act" (Sonnenwald, 1999, p. 184). Sonnenwald describes an information horizon as consisting of a variety of information resources such as social networks, documents, information retrieval tools, and experimentation and observation in the world (1999, p. 185). It can be thought of as sources and channels available to an actor when looking for information. In Agarwal (2011) and Agarwal, Xu, and Poo (2011), I list five types of sources or channels available to an actor engaged in information seeking—face-to-face, phone/chat, email/forum, book/manual, and online. These consist of a combination of synchronous (face-to-face, phone/chat) and asynchronous sources (email/forum), and human (face-to-face, phone/chat, email/forum) and non-human sources (book/manual, online). It is debatable whether information horizon is context, or shaped by the actor's context that gives rise to the information need. In the former case, the sources and channels available to the actor might inform the need for information at a given point in time. In the latter, the actor's context (e.g., at work or in everyday life) gives rise to a need for information, which prompts the actor to look for information from one or more sources i.e., reach out within one's information horizon.

Figure 1.5: Context as information horizon.

Johnson et al. (2006) use the terms fields and pathways, where they define field as the typical arrangement of information stimuli to which the actor is regularly exposed, and the information resources the actor routinely uses (Sonnenwald, 1999; Agarwal Xu, and Poo, 2011). They write that actors are "embedded in a field that acts on them," but that "they also make choices about the nature of their fields, the types of media they attend to, the friendships they form and the neighborhoods they live in…based on their information needs and preferences" (Johnson et al., 2006, p. 571). Johnson et al. define a pathway as the route someone follows in the pursuit of answers to questions—an information matrix formed by a variety of channels, a variety of sources within channels, and a variety of messages contained within these sources. As opposed to an actor's field, Johnson et al. see pathways as "more dynamic and active, focusing on individual actions over-time in response sequences…This movement over-time may result in changing contexts that are the direct result of individual choice and a response to what an individual has uncovered" (p. 572). Thus, while a field is more stable, a pathway depends on what the actor finds and how the actor reacts to this information (Johnson et al., 2006).

g. Context as Constraints

The term *constraints* describes "a host of factors external to the [information seeking] behavior itself" that influence the selection of strategies that people employ to find information. In his "person-as-situation" model, Allen (1997) identifies individual differences and situational factors as acting concurrently to constrain individual or group behavior. "An individual might be able to behave in a certain manner, but will be constrained by the realities of the situation to avoid such behavior. Similarly, a situation might permit several courses of action, but a specific individual might lack the knowledge or abilities necessary to complete one of more of those possible courses of action" (Allen, 1997, p. 119). A group would similarly be constrained by organizational and social values, as well as group dynamics, and their collective knowledge and abilities when faced with certain situations.

In the systems approach terminology, constraints affect information behavior, but cannot be changed by it (Churchman, 1979). However, from a person-centric point of view, the actor is also able to influence context. This is supported by Ingwersen and Järvelin (2005): "actors and other components function as context to one another in the interaction processes" (p. 19). Fidel and Pejtersen's (2004) dimensions of cognitive work analysis (work environment/domain, organization, activity/task, actor's characteristics, resources and values, etc.) each create a constraint for the dimensions nested below them. Brézillon describes context as "what constrains problem solving without intervening in it explicitly" (Brézillon, 1999, p. 48).

h. Context as Life-world/Information World

Chatman (1996), Talja (1997), Lievrouw (2001), and Kari and Savolainen (2003) investigate the role of the actor's life world and information world in shaping the actor's information needs and behavior. "The person's life-world imports the perceived reality in which his/her/their activities take place…some salient attributes of the ordinary life-world are the actor's perceived demographics, personality, way of life, world-view, values and purpose in life" (Kari and Savolainen, 2003, p. 159). Kari and Savolainen also say that humans have the capacity to change their worlds. I would posit that whether certain information sources are a part of an actor's information horizon (Sonnenwald, 1999) or not would also be shaped by the actor's life world.

i. Context as Common Ground and Ordinariness

Common ground is "the information, knowledge and beliefs, which a group (of two or more) have in common and their awareness that the group has this information and knowledge in common" (Sonnenwald, 2006)—in other words, it forms part of the social context. Clark (1996) describes common ground as an important element in human communication and people's use of language, where he describes using language as "dancing a waltz, playing a piano duet or making love, in that they are all kinds of joint action" (Carston, 1999, p. 167). The goal of language use is to increase common ground. Common ground is considered context, especially as it relates to information seeking by an actor from a human source, and the sharing of knowledge by the source with the actor. As Sonnenwald (2006) writes, the "goal of information sharing is to change a person's image of the world and to develop a shared working understanding. It is an essential component of collabora-tion" (abstract). The degree to which a conversation is successful can be measured by the degree to which the parties to the conversation share a common ground, i.e., how much they understand each other. Common ground is something we often assume as given, in our social interactions, but is also something we intuitively work at—through verbal and non-verbal language—through smiles, text messaging, emoticons, acknowledging, emotionally reaching out, etc. Common ground can relate to ordinariness described by Dourish (2004), and first proposed by Harvey Sacks (1984) in his paper "On Doing 'Being Ordinary'", where he analyzed conversations to uncover the unnoticed mecha-nisms by which people would manage the conversation as it proceeded. Being ordinary is an accom-plishment and something that people work at (Dourish, 2004). Dourish describes ordinariness as "something that we do; rather than simply being a stable feature of the world, it is actively managed and achieved in the course of interaction"; "this is a mutual achievement; ordinariness must be both produced and recognized by the parties to an interaction."; "it is relative to particular communities and activities; it is a feature of forms of competent language use for groups of language users" (p. 24). Ordinariness (and common ground) relates to context because, "like ordinariness, context is managed moment by moment, achieved by those carrying out some activity together, and relative to that activity and to the forms of action and engagement that it entails" (p. 25).

j. Context as Discourse

In the social constructionist viewpoint, unlike the cognitive viewpoint, one's entire understanding of the world and way of thinking is based on interaction with other people. I would posit that discourse is usually verbal, while interaction is a broader set of possibilities that include verbal interchanges. Here, discourses set "the boundaries of social knowledge" and act as "repositories of starting points, definitions, and themes that position speakers as they give meanings to phenomena" (Talja, Tuominen, and Savolainen, 2005, p. 89). Thus, the actor's social interaction and discourse helps shape large parts of the actor's information behavior. Savolainen (2012) investigated the contexts in which information need is triggered. One of the three ways in which he describes need is triggered is through dialogue. Context as discourse also relates to the ordinariness of everyday conversation studied by Sacks (1984).

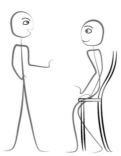

Figure 1.6: **Context as discourse.**

k. Context as Information Ground

Information ground relates to the idea of context as place or social setting (Fisher, Landry, and Naumer, 2006). Writing as Pettigrew (1999), Fisher applied Tuominen and Savolainen's (1997) social constructionist approach and proposed information grounds to describe social settings in which people share everyday information while attending to a focal activity (see Fisher, Durrance, and Hinton, 2004; Fisher et al., 2005; Fisher, Landry, and Naumer, 2006). This grew from her study of everyday information sharing among nurses and the elderly at community foot clinics in Canada. Pettigrew (1999) defined information grounds as synergistic "environment[s] temporarily created when people come together for a singular purpose but from whose behaviour emerges a social atmosphere that fosters the spontaneous and serendipitous sharing of information" (p. 811). According to some of her propositions that she tested empirically (Fisher, Landry, and Naumer, 2006): people gather at "information grounds" for a primary, instrumental purpose other than information sharing; social interaction is a primary activity at "information grounds" such that information flow is a by-product; information grounds can occur anywhere, in any type of temporal setting and are predicated on the presence of individuals; people use information obtained at "information grounds'" in alternative ways, and benefit along physical, social, affective and cognitive dimensions; many sub-contexts exist within an "information ground" and are based on people's perspectives and physical factors; together these sub-contexts form a grand context (Fisher, Durrance, and Hinton, 2004).

1. Context as Assigned Meanings During Interaction

Dourish (2004) recommends turning our attention away from context as a set of descriptive features of settings to practice as forms of engagement with those settings. He writes that, by doing so, we assign a central role to the meanings that people find in the world, and the meanings of their actions for themselves and for others. These meanings are open-ended; part of what people are doing when they adopt and adapt technologies, incorporating them into their own work, is creating and communicating new meanings though those technologies as their working practices evolve. Thus, users, and not designers, determine the meaning of the technologies that they use, through the ways in which they incorporate them into practice (Dourish, 2004, p. 28). Traxler's (2011) summary of Dourish (2004)'s viewpoint is quite apt. Rather than viewing context as information, Dourish defines context as "a relational property" between the actor and other objects or activities, and thus signifies relevance; rather than delineated and defined in advance, context is defined dynamically; rather than stable, context is local to each occasion of activity or action; rather than context and content [or the actor] being two separable entities, "context arises from the activity" or task. Context isn't just "there", but is actively produced, maintained, and enacted in the course of the activity at hand (Dourish, 2004, p. 22; Traxler, 2011). Cook (2010) also mentions the notion of 'user-generated context', which emphasizes the role of the actor and learner in shaping their own context, and erodes the distinction between the actor and the environment (Traxler, 2011). With respect to smartphone use, Natarajan, Shin, and Dhillon (2013) write that the application the actor will launch next intuitively depends on the sequence of apps used recently in the current context. They describe the sequence of clicks made in the current session as interactional context.

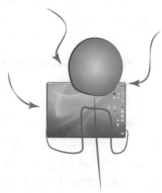

Figure 1.7: Context as assigned meanings during interaction.

m. Context as Proximity and Relevance

Something is generally more likely to be considered part of context if it is proximate to the actor along a particular dimension or for a particular purpose (Guha and Lenat, 1994). Proximity can also relate to time and history. Lee (2011) writes that there is a rough correlation between something being part of the context and its relative recency (proximity in time to the actor). Context can be proximity and relevance, and be "difference and change; it can be seen as a description of that which differentiates, what is different in what is near or recent and what is further or earlier in relation to the subject" (Traxler, 2011, p. 4).

n. Context as Time and Place/Embodiment and Portability

Apart from the idea of working on a task in a specific room in a workplace, or studying for exams in a room, you can also shift context as you read a book in the library, walk out of the library while reading, and continue reading as you board the bus home. Here, the book is portable, and the surrounding environment and people where the actor is embodied is shifting as the actor moves from place to place, while still engaging in the task of reading. This is more apparent now as more and more people carry smartphones, and are seen walking about with their heads focused down on their phones. "Whereas [an actor working on] the desktop computer imposes quite a rigid and separate set of contexts on a user or learner—they are either learning or they are doing something else equally specific –, mobiles produce or enforce a more fragmentary and transient movement between multiple user-contexts." "Real and virtual spaces and the contexts that they represent become interwoven … the user works now in overlapping and fragmentary contexts, where other roles or contexts can easily intrude. Users are no longer dedicated learners nor are there stable contexts" (Traxler, 2011, p. 6). Research on mobile devices tends to focus on this conceptualization of context as time and place because it is easy to automatically capture time and place with mobile devices.

Figure 1.8: Context as portability.

With the increasing usage of social media, *context collapse* (when disparate social networks overlap) has emerged as an important topic (Davis and Jurgenson, 2014; Litt and Hargittai, 2016).

This collapsing of context blurs the public and private, professional and personal, and the many different selves and situation in which individuals find themselves, leading to potentially beneficial as well as problematic consequences (Davis and Jurgenson, 2014). Nissenbuam (2010) proposes the concept of *contextual integrity* as a privacy framework that avoids dichotomies of public and private, and rests instead upon the appropriate practices for collection and dissemination of information rooted in the particular norms governing any given arena. Applying Nissenbuam's framework, Davis and Jurgenson (2014) argue that context collapse happens under varying conditions, depending on the degree of intentionality—when actors collapse contexts on purpose, and when contexts collapse by default or by surprise. They call the first collusions, and the second collisions. Davis and Jurgenson (2014, p. 480) define *context collusions* as "the purposeful, intentional, bringing together of various contexts and their related networks," like inviting close friends, distant relatives and more to a wedding. Through a two-month-long diary study of 119 diverse American adults and their 1,200 social network site posts, followed by 30 interviews, Litt and Hargittai (2016) explore the imagined audience on social network sites (the people constituted under "collusions"). Davis and Jurgenson (2014) define *context collisions* as "those occasions in which contexts come together without any effort on the part of the actor, and sometimes, unbeknownst to the actor, with potentially chaotic results" (p. 481) or the violation of privacy rules under the condition of collapsing contexts (Davis and Jurgenson, 2014).

o. Context as Legacy and Determinant

The cultural-historical perspective views context as the legacy of past activities and as a determinant of present activities (Allen, Karanasios, and Slavova, 2011). Here, "context is viewed simultaneously as a byproduct and a determinant of history, embedded in action. The present context is a result of the social pressures of the past and past actions, giving rise to current practices and meanings, and it creates a cultural environment that impacts on the available courses of action for the future" (Allen, Karanasios, and Slavova, 2011, p. 783). Here, we can understand context as the set of circumstances of the past, and how the actor(s) reacted to them (by engaging in information behavior), which give rise to circumstances of the present (the present context as viewed by the actor) that will inform the actor's reactions and choices in information behavior. These reactions and choices/behavior, in turn, create or influence the context for the actor and other actors connected to or affected by the person.

1.3   CHAPTER SUMMARY

In this chapter, we briefly looked at the research field of information behavior. We saw the difficulty in trying to define context, and discussed the many definitions and types of context that researchers have studied. Thus, context could be an environment or container, a setting, a role, a situation, the actor's mind, information horizon/field and pathways, constraint, life world/information world, common ground and ordinariness, discourse, information ground, interaction, proximity and relevance, time, place, embodiment and portability, or legacy and determinant. This listing of types of context described above is important, but not exhaustive. Different researchers use different set of terms to distinguish context types. Schmidt, Beigl, and Gellesen (1998) distinguish between context relating to human factors and context relating to the physical environment. Chen and Kotz (2000) propose four categories of contexts: computing context, physical context, user context and time context. Ingwersen and Järvelin (2005) describe organizational, social, and cultural context. Here, the organizational context is closer to context as setting, and the social context has similarities with common ground, discourse, and information ground discussed above. Lee (2011, p. 99) also lists taxonomies of context proposed by different researchers. Fidel (2012) distinguishes fluid and dynamic context from identifiable and stable context. She also makes a distinction between real vs. perceived context. Ingwersen and Järvelin (2005) nest the information retrieval context within the seeking context, which, in turn, is nested within the work task context, which is nested within the socio-organizational context.

What we have discussed (and is of interest in this book) is the context of an actor when interacting with information. The study of context itself can be approached from many perspectives, "such as the context surrounding documents, the context influencing actors and tasks, [and] the context affecting interaction and its instances of implicit and explicit relevance feedback" (description of first IIiX). Lee (2011) describes a framework on contextual information in digital collections. While researchers have most talked about the context influencing actors and tasks, the other perspectives of context can all affect the actor. For example, the context surrounding information sources (e.g., Agarwal, 2011; Agarwal, Xu, and Poo, 2011) does affect the actor's information horizon (Sonnenwald, 1999) when looking for information.

In the next chapter, we will review the literature on the influence of context of information behavior. This comprehensive review will help us determine what has happened in the field—as it relates to context—thus far. This will be useful as I put forward my own thinking on context in Chapters 3, 4, and 5, where we map the conceptual space and finally arrive at a definition for context.

CHAPTER 2

Literature Review: The Influence of Context on Information Behavior

So far, we have looked at the many definitions and types of context within the field of information behavior—context as environment or container, context as setting, context as role, context as situation, context as the actor's mind, context as information horizon/field and pathways, context as constraints, context as life world/information world, context as common ground and ordinariness, context as discourse, context as information ground, context as assigned meanings during interaction, context as proximity and relevance, context as time, place, embodiment and portability, and context as legacy and determinant.

In this chapter, we will review the literature pertaining to context and its influence on human information behavior. We will start by reviewing several influential models and frameworks of information behavior that have incorporated context. We will then examine empirical studies on information seeking and other forms of information behavior where context has played an important part. I group the studies based on populations studied, methods used, variables studied, and the application of context in information retrieval. While the definitions and types that we saw in Chapter 1 were theoretical conceptions of context, the variables we examine in this chapter are more concrete in the way they were incorporated in empirical studies. We will also map these theoretical conceptions to different contextual elements that we examine in this chapter, such as actor, task, source, etc.

2.1 MODELS AND FRAMEWORKS INCORPORATING CONTEXT

When individual researchers created these models, they may not always have used the term context explicitly. However, their frameworks use terms that we understand as context or part of context. I have highlighted these in blue in the figures in this section. In certain figures—multiple shades of blue are used. The different shades are used for stylistic purposes and to make it easier to discern the different parts of the particular figure. Each shade simply denotes context. The blue highlighting can help us see how different models and frameworks have addressed context. In all cases, we recognize context (the parts in blue) as the factors that affect information behavior, as this is our focus in this book. I have left unshaded any form of information behavior in the figures (denoting some action such as seeking, processing, using, evaluating, or an outcome of that action). However,

Ingwersen and Järvelin (2005) argued that everything is a context to everything else. Thus, it could be argued that the information behavior, in turn, affects the other contextual factors, and serves as a context for those factors.

Beginning in the early 1980s, Tom Wilson proposed a series of models that reflects the evolution in information seeking research. Figure 2.1 below shows Wilson's major model (Wilson and Walsh, 1996). In this model, he explicitly recognizes the context that gives rise to the person's information need, and he clearly sees the person as being situated within this context. I'd posit that the activating mechanisms and intervening variables in his model, while not labeled as context, are still part of the context that influences the person's decision to seek information and specific seeking activities. These are all shaded in blue.

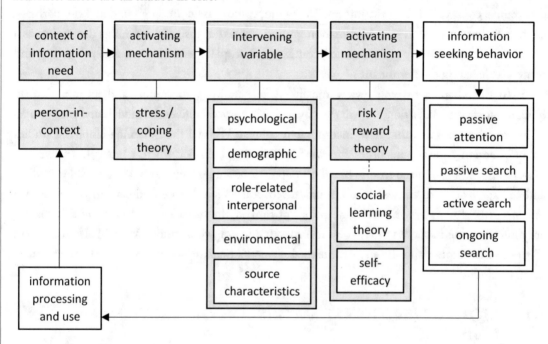

Figure 2.1: Context in Wilson and Walsh's (1996) model.

Kuhlthau's (1993) model shows a series of stages that form part of a person's information search process (Figure 2.2). These include the feelings (affective), thoughts (cognitive), and actions (actual behavior) of a person during different stages of looking for information, with the initial confusion and vagueness giving way to greater clarity as the person perseveres with the search. Here, the task stage can be seen as a particular situation at different points in time, giving rise to differing information needs during the respective stages. The tasks, feelings, and thoughts here all comprise context.

Tasks	Initiation	Selection	Exploration	Formula-tion	Collection	Presentation	Assessment
Feelings (affective)	uncertainty	optimism	confusion frustration doubt	clarity	sense of direction / confidence	satisfaction or disap-pointment	sense of accomplish-ment
Thoughts (cognitive)	vague			focused			increased self-awareness
Actions (physical)		seeking relevant information			seeking pertinent information		
		exploring ⟶ documenting					

Figure 2.2: Context in Kuhlthau's (1993) model of the information search process.

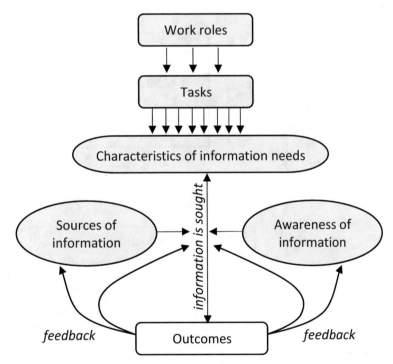

Figure 2.3: Context in Leckie, Pettigrew, and Sylvain (1996).

The Leckie, Pettigrew, and Sylvain (1996) model pertains to organizational information seeking, with work roles and tasks as part of the model (see Figure 2.3). Here, work roles, tasks, characteristics of information needs, sources of information, and awareness of information all comprise the context that affects the person's information seeking behavior in a workplace. In describing characteristics of information needs, Leckie et al. write that the actor's information need, while arising out of situations pertaining to a specific task associated with one or more work roles of the actor, is not constant, and can be influenced by a number of intervening factors. These factors could be individiual demographics, internally or externally prompted situation, frequency—recurring need or new, predictability—anticipated or unexpected need, importance—degrees of urgency, and complexity—easily resolved or difficult (Leckie et al., 1996, pp. 182-183).

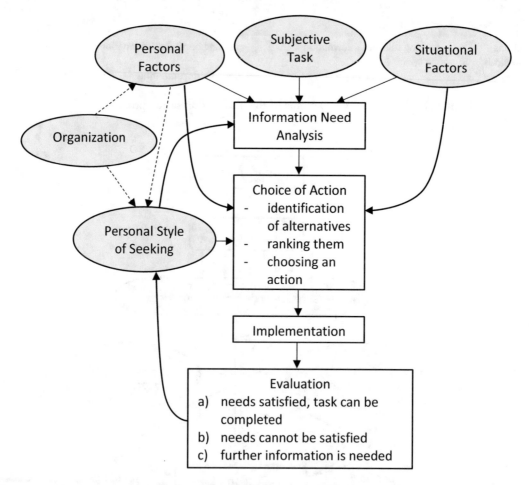

Figure 2.4: Context in Byström and Järvelin (1995).

Byström and Järvelin (1995) categorized organizational tasks into five complexity classes and classified information, sources, and channels into types. Their model includes a number of factors (see Figure 2.4)—subjective task, personal factors (e.g., age, education, experience, attitude, motivation, and mood), situational factors (e.g., time available for performing the task), organization, and personal style of seeking, which all comprise the context that gives rise to information need and leads to information seeking behavior. Here, actor variables such as the actor's age, education, experience, etc. and personal style of seeking can be seen to be relatively stable aspects of the context, as compared to more dynamic aspects such as motivation and mood.

The information retrieval literature has cited the model as a useful way of thinking about the way information users operate (Case and Given, 2016). The model draws attention to the effects of "task complexity" in information seeking (denoted by "subjective tasks" in the figure); how a user proceeds depends on the degree to which they see the task as complicated (Case and Given, 2016). Research models often incorporate the term variable, which is any object or idea that can be measured in the course of the study. Trochim (2006), Salkind (2010), and MacKinnon (2011) discuss different types of variables. In Byström and Järvelin's model, organization, subjective task and situation factors are independent variables. These types of variables are denoted by arrows coming out of them but not going into them. Thus, they affect other variables but are not affected by any other. Personal factors and personal style of seeking are mediating variables with both arrows coming into and going out of them. All these contextual variables (shaded in blue) affect other mediating and dependent variables (the outcome or effect in a cause-effect relationship).

Savolainen (1995) provides a detailed model of a person's everyday life information seeking behavior surrounded by context. Almost everything in the model (Figure 2.5) can be seen as context. The outermost box of "everyday life" is context to the "way of life"—time budget, consumption models and hobbies of the information seeker—which affects and is affected by the "mastery of life"—approaches one chooses to solve problems and to keep things in order. All of these are affected by values, money, social contacts, culture, life situation, etc. Within this context of mastery of life are specific projects of everyday life, problematic situations to deal with, and situational factors, all of which affect problem solving behavior. These elements in Savolainen's model can be considered different types and levels of context. The model is less causal than other flowchart-like or task-based information seeking models, and takes a long-term view of one's information seeking behavior when going about everyday tasks like shopping, taking care of the home, pursuing hobbies, etc.

Elfreda Chatman (1991, 1992, 1996) conducted a series of ethnographic studies which resulted in theories of information poverty, life in the round, and normative behavior. She incorporated context as "small worlds" to study the information behavior of underserved and marginalized populations. She discovered four critical concepts that serve as the basis for defining an impoverished life-world of outsiders: risk-taking, secrecy, deception, and situational relevance (Chatman, 1996). These four factors affect information poverty. The life world (which we understand as context), in turn, affects all the interaction the user has with information. Chatman's theories highlighted two different worlds - the world of the information poor or outsiders, and the world of the insiders. We can deduce that there is a distinction between the context of the insider, and the context of the marginalized outsider, which was the focus of Chatman's studies.

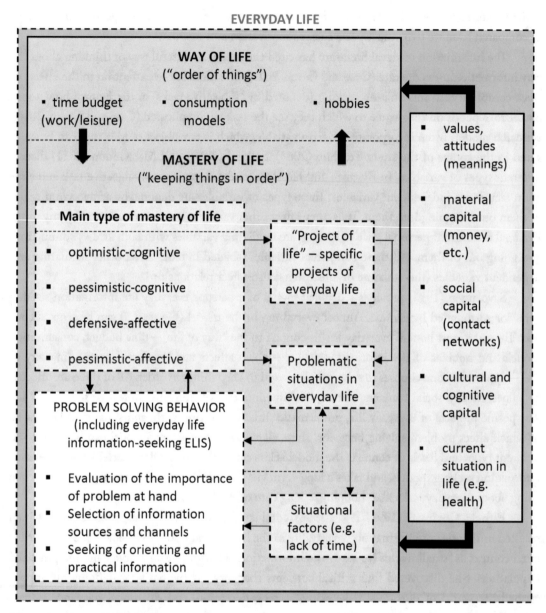

Figure 2.5: Context in Savolainen (1995).

Sonnenwald (1999) defines context as "the quintessence of a set (or group) of past, present and future situations," with "some shared understanding of a context by its participants," which she says need not be identical or complete (p. 178). As an example of boundaries of context that are open to negotiation, she describes writing research papers as being within the boundaries of academic context but outside the boundaries of family life context. Context can be described by a variety of dimensions or attributes such as place, time, goals, tasks, systems, situations, processes, organizations and types of participants (Sonnenwald, 1999, p. 179). She describes situation as a set of related activities, or a set of related stories, that occurs over time, and that arises within a given context. A context may consist of a variety of situations. Situations from one context may overlap with situations from another context, e.g., an academic, when grading papers (work context) gets a call from a spouse and discusses a family situation (family context) (p. 180). Sonnenwald's conceptualization of context as different from situation is a good example of the challenges in finding a shared meaning and definition of context, and why it has remained a "slippery notion" (Dourish, 2004, p. 29).

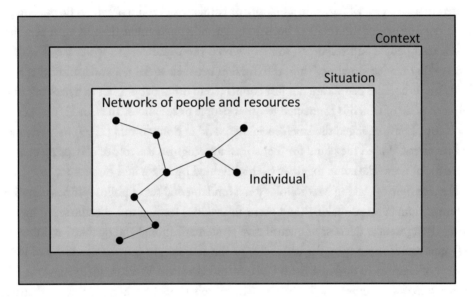

Figure 2.6: Context in Sonnenwald (1999).

Social network refers to a structure of communication among individuals. These networks help construct situations and contexts, and are constructed by situations and contexts (Sonnenwald, 1999, p. 180). With the rise of social media, the overlapping of disparate social networks, and the privacy implications that come with it has led to terms such as context collapse (Davis and Jurgenson, 2014; Litt and Hargittai, 2016). Figure 2.6 shows a social network (network of people) within a given situation that occurs within a broader context. Some members of the social network are part of the situation, but others may be outside it. Here, we see the individual, the social network, situation and the broader "context" (as used by Sonnenwald), all as different elements of context. These are, thus, shaded in the figure. Sonnenwald proposes that within a context and a situation is an information horizon in which a person can look for information. An information horizon may consist of a variety of information resources, such as social networks, including colleagues, subject matter experts, reference librarians, information brokers, etc.; documents, including broadcast media, web pages, and books; information retrieval tools, including computer-based information retrieval systems, bibliographies, etc.; and experimentation and observation in the world. Information horizons, and subsequently information resources, are determined socially and individually for situations and contexts. (Sonnenwald, 1999, p. 185).

It is a little perplexing why Sonnenwald chose to include an individual with need as part of a social network, but didn't include other impersonal sources of information (such as documents, tools, websites, etc.) as equally connected resources forming a "web of things," some of which are connected to a given social network, situation, or context, and some of which lie outside of a given situation or context. An information horizon of an individual could then be seen as a network of interconnected people and resources, some of which the user refers to when faced with an information-seeking task or situation. Thus, the division between social networks and other resources is artificial. This is because people are not just connected to other people, but to a network of resources as well, each node of which is connected to other people or resources. Thus, in Figure 2.6, to achieve greater clarity, I have changed the label "social network" in Sonnenwald (1999) to "networks of people and resources." I used the plural for "networks" to recognize the role of collapsing contexts when disparate social networks come together (as highlighted by Davis and Jurgenson, 2014).

Dervin's Sense-Making Methodology is a fundamental set of philosophic assumptions about the nature of human sense-making (and sense-unmaking) leading to a specific set of methodological moves trying to take the best of quantitative (systematizations) and qualitative (interpretive and critical) approaches to studying the user, actor or the audience in communication, and is applicable to a variety of contexts in different fields (Dervin and Foreman-Wernet, 2012; Agarwal, 2012). Her model recognizes the actor as a "body-mind-heart-spirit moving through time and space, with a past history, present reality and future dreams or ambitions" (Foreman-Wernet, 2003, p. 7). Dervin sees human communication as sense-making and sense-unmaking, which she conceptualizes as gap bridging within a moment in time and space, with a new moment requiring new gap-bridging (Figure 2.7). While the gap-bridging may change with time, at a given moment, the actor is anchored in a particular situation and context, which leads to a gap (need, questions, confusions) that the actor may try to fill from one or more sources. While Dervin's conception of context in the model is limited to social and organizational factors (see the context umbrella in Figure 2.7), these factors, along with the actor, situation, gaps, bridges, sources, and relevances, can all be considered context of information behavior. Some attributes of the actor, gap, bridge and source may be relatively more stable (e.g., age, gender, etc.) than other attributes (e.g., thoughts, emotions) affecting the actor's sense-making and un-making in time and space.

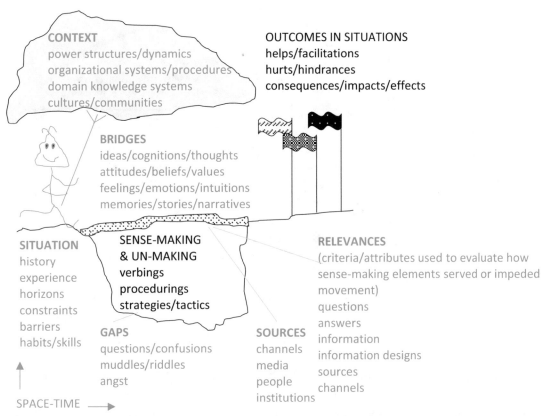

Figure 2.7: Context in Dervin's Sense-Making Methodology's central metaphor (Dervin and Fore-man-Wernet, 2012).

Pamela McKenzie's (2003) model focuses on the social aspect of information practices in everyday life, as opposed to the cognitive aspect of information seeking or behavior in work life (Figure 2.8). The model considers the different modes that the actor could be in, and the information behaviors that result from them. These range from active information seeking to being referred through an intermediary to encountering information serendipitously. As opposed to a number of other models that focus exclusively on information seeking behavior, this model sees information seeking as one of several types of information practices or behaviors that an individual engages in in everyday life. The model recognizes the individual as part of a larger context (as also in Wilson and Walsh, 1996). In McKenzie's (2003) qualitative study, the participants were nineteen Canadian women pregnant with twins, who were initially interviewed and then telephoned twice in a week to inquire about critical incidents. Thus, the factors affecting the information practices in everyday life (studied for a week) of these women formed the context in McKenzie's study, which informed her model.

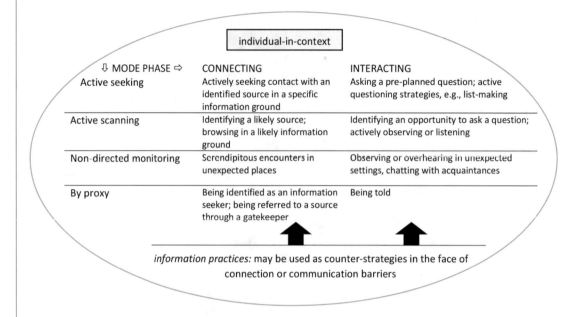

Figure 2.8: Context in McKenzie's (2003) two-dimensional model of information practices.

While information seeking is the most often-studied type of information behavior, there are times when people choose to avoid or stop seeking information. Sweeny et al. (2010) define information avoidance as any behavior designed to prevent or delay the acquisition of available but potentially unwanted information. It can entail asking someone not to reveal information, physically leaving a situation to avoid learning information, or simply failing to take the necessary steps to reveal the content of information. Sweeny et al. point out that information avoidance can be temporary (with the intention of learning the information later) or permanent. In an age when people are connected actively to a huge number of other people through social media and through smartphones and messaging apps, information avoidance (or avoidance of people) could manifest itself almost every day, when one or more person(s) do not respond to a sender's emails, messages or phone calls, or do not respond within the expected timeframe of the sender.

Sweeny et al.'s framework (Figure 2.9) includes individual differences and situational factors that affect the actor's motivation to either seek, allow, or avoid information. They conclude that people may be motivated to avoid information because the information might threaten their cherished beliefs about themselves, others or the world (threats to beliefs); the information might demand undesired change or action (obligations to act); or the information or the decision to learn might lead to unpleasant emotions (regulating emotions). In the model, individual differences, situational factors and motivations can all be seen as contextual factors that affect the actor's information (avoidance) behavior. The actor's individual differences would be relatively stable aspects of the context affecting the decision to seek or avoid information. In the figure, individual differences and situational factors are independent variables, while motivations is a mediating variable. The information avoiding or seeking decision is the outcome or dependent variable.

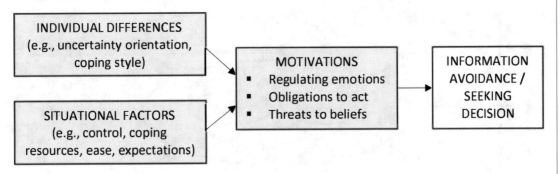

Figure 2.9: Sweeny et al. (2010)'s framework for understanding information avoidance decisions.

While the models we have discussed thus far have taken the point of the view of the individual actor and their information behavior, Karunakaran, Reddy, and Spence's (2013) model (Figure 2.10) deals with the behavior of a group of people working together. The model focuses on the phenomenon of collaborative information seeking in organizations. Karunakaran et al. define collaborative information behavior as an umbrella term to connote the collaborative aspects of information seeking, retrieval, and use. They conceptualize it as comprised of a set of constitutive activities, organized into three broad phases—problem formulation, collaborative information seeking, and information use. Whereas in individual seeking the trigger for the decision to seek is a lack of information and a gap between the current situation and future tasks or demands, in collaborative information behavior, triggers could be complexity of information need, fragmented information resources, lack of domain expertise, or lack of immediately accessible information. Communication between the participants plays a central role.

The model recognizes a situation that arises within an organizational context, for which collaborative information behavior is required. Here, the triggers that give rise to the need, the shared representation of the problem, unmet needs and a shared understanding achieved are all contextual factors that affect the group's collaborative information sharing, searching and retrieving behavior. The model recognizes that the result of one round of seeking action (unmet needs and shared understanding until that point) becomes the context for the next round of seeking action by the collaborating group.

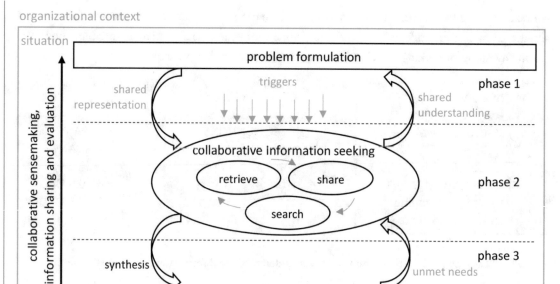

Figure 2.10: Context in Karunakaran, Reddy, and Spence's (2013) model of collaborative information behavior in organizations.

Jumisko-Pyykkö and Vainio's (2010) model focuses on context as it pertains to mobile computing and mobile human-computer interaction (Figure 2.11). It lists components of context (physical, temporal, task, social, and technical and information context), and subcomponents for each, as well as properties that would apply across the different types or components of context (level of magnitude, dynamism, pattern and typical combinations).

The physical context describes the apparent features of situation in which the human-mobile computer interaction takes place. The temporal context describes the actor's interaction with the mobile computer (mobile system or device—for example, smartphones or tablets) in relation to time. The task context describes the surrounding tasks in relation to the actor's task of interacting with the mobile system. It is related to the demands of the entire situation upon one's attention. In their conceptual framework for tasks in information studies, Byström and Hansen (2005) suggest that work task contain one or several information seeking tasks or sub-tasks, and that each information seeking task contains one or more information search tasks. In Jumisko-Pyykkö and Vainio's model, the social context describes the other people present, their characteristics and roles, the interpersonal interactions and the surrounding culture that influence the actor's interaction with a mobile system. The technical context describes the relationship of other relevant systems and services to the actor's interaction with the system.

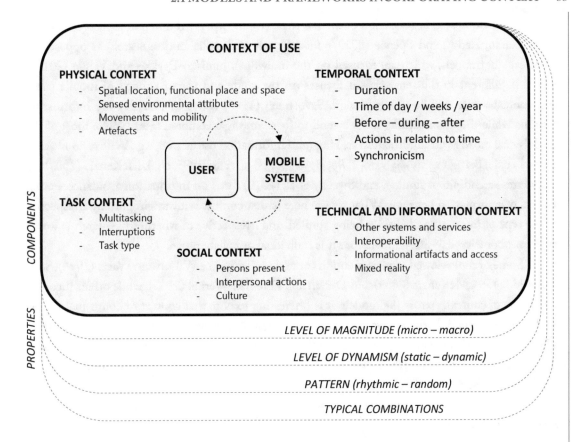

Figure 2.11: Jumisko-Pyykkö and Vainio (2010)'s model of Context of Use in Human-Mobile Computer Interaction (CoU-HMCI).

Jumisko-Pyykkö and Vainio (2010) describe the role of properties as helping to perceive the central structures and regularity among the broad list of components and subcomponents of context and to underline the dynamism between the modular descriptions of context. For example, *macro* or *micro* pertain to the lens of viewing context, where a nearby object would be part of the micro context, and an object far away would be macro. The things that remain mostly constant over time (e.g., one's office space, time of browsing, etc.) are static, while things that change, e.g., the webpage one is reading, is dynamic. Contextual components can follow a rhythmic pattern or could be random. Space and time (physical and temporal components) are an example of a combination of contextual components that occur together.

What we've seen is a selection of models that have incorporated different aspects of context. Karunakaran, Reddy, and Spence (2013)'s model deals with collaborative search, as opposed to other seeking models, which are focused on the individual. Jumisko-Pyykkö and Vainio (2010)'s model is different in the sense that it focuses on the study and use of context of mobile usage and context-aware mobile-system design. Savolainen (1995) concerns everyday-life information seeking, while the other seeking models tend to focus on organizational tasks. While most of the models deal mostly with information seeking (and information use as well, e.g., Wilson and Walsh, 1996; Leckie, Pettigrew, and Sylvain, 1996; Byström and Järvelin, 1995, etc.), McKenzie (2003) incorporates serendipitous finding, and Sweeny et al. (2010) focus on information avoidance—other aspects of information behavior. What we see here is that context is always important, irrespective of the type of information behavior being studied, and irrespective of whether the search is work-task-based or everyday-life, and whether it is individual or collaborative.

Some of the reviewed models mention context explicitly, like Wilson and Walsh (1996), Sonnenwald (1999), McKenzie (2003) and Dervin and Foreman-Wernet (2012), while others incorporate facets of context. Across the models, it is interesting to note that context or contextual factors are found on the periphery, i.e., they either surround other factors or lead to specific outcomes. Thus, a large number of contextual factors act as either independent, mediating, or moderating variables that affect other variables by their presence. Thus, the outcome (for instance, of the search process) would have been different if one or more contextual variables were not present.

Let us now look at contextual variables that have been a part of empirical studies in information behavior.

2.2   EMPIRICAL STUDIES INCORPORATING CONTEXT

The Information Seeking in Context (ISIC) and Information Interaction in Context (IIiX) conferences have been at the forefront of research into how context shapes information behavior, and how context might be incorporated into the design of retrieval systems. As such, they provide a wide array of empirical studies on context. I drew upon all the available published proceedings from both conferences, as well as other library and information science journals and conference proceedings, where appropriate, for the following review.

The ISIC and IIiX/CHIIR studies included in this section examined contextual factors for either causation or, at least, correlation, i.e., they showed how context affects other factors or outcomes. More importantly, most of these studies examined how context affects the focus of the particular studies, i.e., some type of information behavior or practice. Only a few studies incorporate more complex models of cause and effect. While studies from all proceedings over the years were reviewed, those included are relevant studies from the past five years (2012–2017) from ISIC and IIiX/CHIIR. Older studies from these conferences, and also from other library and information science journals and conference proceedings, were included when they were of particular interest e.g., when they incorporated multiple contextual variables. Studies excluded from this review were either theoretical studies or position papers, studies on the design of information retrieval systems using context (although I discuss these in Section 2.2.4 below), and studies that looked at people within a specific role or environment but did not explicitly show effects of specific context variables. Looking for causal relationships is important because it demonstrates the importance of context in affecting (or not affecting) behavior.

In reviewing the studies, it is useful to first examine the populations that were studied, and the types of research methods used in those studies. We will then go into the details of different types of context variables examined in these studies that affected a particular type of information behavior.

2.2.1 POPULATIONS STUDIED

Table 2.1 lists studies that have looked at different segments of the population when investigating context in information behavior. These include studies on members of various professions, such as doctors, bankers, engineers/IT workers, librarians, researchers, marketing professionals, government workers, and pharmaceutical workers. Researchers have also studied people in different roles such as administrators and managers, hobbyists, and university students. As can be seen from the number of studies listed, university students are a frequently studied population. This is because much research is carried out by faculty and Ph.D. students in university settings, where they find it easier to obtain access to the student population as participants in research.

Other studies pertaining to a specific demographic include those on dyslexic students, children and members of the general public. The populations investigated in prior studies relate to the actor variables that we will discuss in Section 2.2.3. Much of what is discussed here is about the actor's profession, domain, or role. All these are relatively stable aspects of the actor. The assumption in these studies is that this attribute of the actor makes a difference in how they approach human-information interaction.

Table 2.1: Population studied in research studies investigating context in information behavior		
	Population Studied	**Source(s)**
Professions	Doctors	Abad-Garcia, Gonzalez-Teruel, and Sanjuan-Nebot (1999)
	Bankers	Allen and Wilson (2003)
	Engineers / IT workers	Bruce et al. (2003); Kiseleva et al. (2016)
	Librarians	Suorsa and Huotari (2014); Bailey and Kelly (2016)
	Researchers	Barry (1997); Anderson (2005); Bartlett, Ishimura, and Kloda (2011)
	Marketing professionals	Du et al. (2013)
	Government workers	Berryman (2006, 2008)
	Pharma company employees	Algon (1997)
Roles	Administrators / Managers	Byström (1997); Dixon and Banwell (1999); Mackenzie (2005); Saastamoinen, Kumpulainen, and Järvelin (2012)
	University students	Steinerová (2008); Joho, Hannah, and Jose (2008); Askola, Atsushi, and Huotari (2010); Bronstein (2010); Liu et al. (2010); Hughes-Morgan and Wilson (2012); Pharo and Nordlie (2012); Ishimura and Bartlett (2013); Pang (2014); Liu et al. (2014); Kim and Sin (2015); Collins-Thompson et al. (2016); Crescenzi, Kelly, and Azzopardi (2016); Edwards and Kelly (2016); Sarrafzadeh et al. (2016); Huurdeman, Wilson, and Kamps (2016)
	Hobbyists	Case (2010)

Demographic	Disability (dyslexic students)	MacFarlane et al. (2012)
	Age (children)	Eickhoff, Dekker, and de Vries (2012); Agarwal (2014)
	No population specified (general public)	Borlund, Dreier, and Byström (2012); Fransson (2012); Mikkonen and Vakkari (2012); Singer, Norbisrath, and Lewandowski (2012); Brennan, Kelly, and Arguello (2014); Gossen, Höbel, and Nürnberger (2014); Schaller, Harvey, and Elsweiler (2014); Enwald et al. (2015); Sun and Zhang (2016)

2.2.2   METHODS USED

Table 2.2 lists the research methods used to investigate context in information behavior. See Case and Given (2016, Chapter 9) for an overview of different methods used to gather data in social science research. As we can see from the table, different researchers have used both quantitative and qualitative methodologies, as well as a mix of different methods in a single study.

Quantitative studies have included surveys and experiments. Surveys are useful for reaching out to large segments of the population in one go. Structured questions also help in relatively quick analysis of the data gathered. Mikkonen and Vakkari (2012) conducted a survey of public library patrons to investigate seeking strategies at the library. Pang (2014) surveyed working students in Singapore to investigate how people look for information during crisis situations.

Online web-based surveys are increasingly used for gathering data. Askola, Atsushi, and Huotari (2010) surveyed Finnish and Japanese university students to investigate their information practices in a health information context. Kim and Sin (2015) surveyed college students to examine how social media sites are used for information seeking. Sun and Zhang (2016) conducted an online survey of the general public to investigate how people look for health information online.

Experiments are useful for manipulating specific causal variables in controlled settings to see if there is any change in the dependent variable. The ecological validity of a study means that the methods, materials and setting of the study must approximate the real world that is being examined (Brewer, 2000). Ecological validity of experimental findings can be low, as these settings may not reflect real-life behavior of the people studied. Many researchers investigating context in information search and retrieval studies have used controlled experiments. The studies listed in this paragraph all utilized university students. Liu et al. (2010) investigated user interaction with content-based image retrieval. Hughes-Morgan and Wilson (2012) conducted a study to compare three search interaction models. MacFarlane et al. (2012) studied the search behavior of dyslexic students. Pharo and

Nordlie (2012) studied task performance in a simulated digital bookstore. Liu et al. (2014) studied the meaning of time constraints to information searchers. Collins-Thompson et al. (2016) carried out a controlled experiment with undergraduate and graduate students to explore how Web search strategies affect students' learning outcomes. Crescenzi, Kelly, and Azzopardi (2016) investigated how time constraints on information seeking affect people's perceptions and behavior. Edwards and Kelly (2016) investigated how interest in a work task affects search behavior and engagement. Huurdeman, Wilson, and Kamps (2016) studied computer science students in an experimental setting, where they applied Kuhlthau's (1991) Information Search Process model to study how search engine use changes at different stages of a task. In an experiment with undergraduate students, Sarrafzadeh et al. (2016) compared two search interfaces—knowledge graphs and hierarchies.

Researchers have conducted experiments outside of the university student population as well. Joho, Hannah, and Jose (2008) conducted an experiment with computer science researchers to compare task performance in individual vs. collaborative searching environments. Kiseleva et al. (2016) studied IT workers to investigate what factors led to user satisfaction with intelligent assistants like Siri and Alexa. Singer, Norbisrath, and Lewandowski (2012) carried out an experiment with members of the general public assessing their difficulty, effort, and outcome in simple and complex search tasks using a search engine. Brennan, Kelly, and Arguello (2014) also studied the general public, investigating how people's cognitive abilities affect their search behavior. Eickhoff, Dekker, and de Vries (2012) conducted an experiment with elementary-school children to study their search behavior. Gossen, Höbel, and Nürnberger (2014) compared children's and adults' search behavior in an experimental setting.

A number of researchers have utilized qualitative methods like interviews and focus groups, ethnography and observation, and content analysis to study context in information behavior.

Interviews are good for answering *how* and *why* questions in research studies. Focus groups allow reaching out to a group of people at once, as compared to interviews, which typically involve talking to one or two people. Abad-Garcia, Gonzalez-Teruel, and Sanjuan-Nebot (1999) carried out personal interviews of physicians in a Spain hospital based on a questionnaire designed using the critical incident technique. Allen and Wilson (2003) utilized individual and group interviews to gather data on the role of organizational climate on information load in a case study of a multinational bank in the UK. Berryman (2006, 2008) used the critical incident technique in semi-structured interviews in a case study of public policy workers. Steinerová (2008) interviewed Ph.D. students to examine what factors impacted their relevance judgments when conducting research. Bailey and Kelly (2016) used interviews and focus groups with librarians to develop a model of factors that affect online search expertise.

Ethnographic studies require the researcher to immerse oneself in the participants' environment over an extended period. Observation is typically a key part of such studies. Barry (1997) used a qualitative, ethnographic approach in a two-year study of theoretical physicists working collectively on a large number of research projects. Anderson (2005) used participant observation of two researchers over a two-year period to create a multi-layered narrative by weaving together different ethnographic stories—impressionist tales along with anecdotes and vignettes—with passages from field notes, e-mail correspondence, video and audio records and other documents associated with their story (para. 13). Building on Sacks (1984), who studied ordinariness in everyday conversation, Dourish (2004) proposes ethnomethodology as an important method for studying and understanding context as arising from interaction.

Observation requires the researcher to simply see without questioning, and to document what one sees. I carried out unstructured, naturalistic observation over two and a half years to study a child's interaction with touch-based devices (Agarwal, 2014). Suorsa and Huotari (2014) used observational methods to study knowledge creation among employees of a children's reading program.

Content analysis requires going through data (documents, artifacts, blog entries, forum posts, journal articles, newspaper clippings, etc.) to look for any interesting patterns. Case (2010) analyzed online forum posts to investigate how coin collectors decide whether to purchase an item for their collection.

The most ambitious studies are the ones that utilize more than one research method. This is known as multimethod research. When a mix of qualitative and quantitative methods is used, it is termed mixed-method research. Multi- or mixed-method research is useful as it helps in triangulation of research findings gathered through one type of method. This approach often takes more time than single-method studies.

Algon (1997) used participant observation, analysis of a critical incident of one task related in response to a survey, and semi-open-ended interviews to study the classification of tasks, steps, and information-related behaviors of individuals in project teams. Using a diary study and interviews, Byström (1997) studied how municipal administrators completed work tasks and made decisions. Dixon and Banwell (1999) investigated the information seeking and decision making of British school governors using a mix of observation, interviews, questionnaires, and documentary analysis. Bruce et al. (2003) studied the collaborative behaviors of design engineers. They conducted interviews and field observation using the cognitive work analysis framework. Using interviews and social network mapping, Mackenzie (2005) investigated how managers choose which coworkers to use as information sources. In her study of library and information science students, Bronstein's (2010) collected data in two ways. The participants wrote a personal diary for two months, and answered an open-ended questionnaire. Bartlett, Ishimura, and Kloda (2011) also conducted a diary study and interviewed researchers to understand what factors influenced their choice of bioinformatics tool.

Borlund, Dreier, and Byström (2012) used both a laboratory experiment and an observational study to examine what affects the amount of time people spend on a search. Saastamoinen, Kumpulainen, and Järvelin (2012) conducted a diary study and observation of city administrators to study how they performed work tasks. Fransson (2012) used log analysis and a questionnaire to study the information seeking behavior of visitors to a digital library. In a study consisting of a questionnaire, diary study and interviews, Du et al. (2013) investigated marketing professionals' source and channel choices. Utilizing interviews and participant-made portfolios and flowcharts, Ishimura and Bartlett (2013) studied the differences in research behaviors and information literacy between Canadian and Japanese college students. Schaller, Harvey, and Elsweiler (2014) used log analysis and questionnaires to study the needs and priorities of app users at a music festival. Enwald et al. (2015) used a questionnaire along with physiological measurements to study the health information preferences of young men in Finland.

Table 2.2: Research methods used in studies investigating context in information behavior

Methodology	Methods used	Source(s)
Quantitative	Surveys	Askola et al. (2010); Mikkonen and Vakkari (2012); Pang (2014); Kim and Sin (2015); Sun and Zhang (2016)
	Experiments	Joho et al. (2008); Liu et al. (2010); Eickhoff et al. (2012); Hughes-Morgan and Wilson (2012); MacFarlane et al. (2012); Pharo and Nordlie (2012); Singer et al. (2012); Brennan et al. (2014); Gossen et al. (2014); Liu et al. (2014); Collins-Thompson et al. (2016); Huurdeman et al. (2016); Sarrafzadeh et al. (2016); Kiseleva et al. (2016)
Qualitative	Interviews / focus groups	Abad-Garcia et al. (1999); Allen and Wilson (2003); Berryman (2006, 2008); Steinerová (2008); Bailey and Kelly (2016)
	Ethnography / Observation	Barry (1997); Anderson (2005); Agarwal (2014); Suorsa and Huotari (2014)
	Content analysis	Case (2010)
Mixed / multi methods		Algon (1997); Byström (1997); Dixon and Banwell (1999); Bruce et al. (2003); Mackenzie (2005); Bronstein (2010); Bartlett et al. (2011); Borlund et al. (2012); Saastamoinen et al. (2012); Fransson (2012); Du et al. (2013); Ishimura and Bartlett (2013); Schaller et al. (2014); Enwald et al. (2015)

2.2.3   VARIABLES STUDIED

I grouped the variables studied into categories: those relating to the type of information behavior studied (the dependent or outcome variable affected by context), the actor's environment, the task and/or situation, the information need and/or specific information required, the actor (also called the person or the user), the information source, the relationship between the actor and the source, and time/space. I chose these categories as they help uniquely group most of the variables found in empirical studies (as well as theoretical models) incorporating context. Of these, many of the variables relating to the actor (e.g., demographics) and to the source point to more stable attributes of context. We can also find many of these context categories in earlier reviews on context in information behavior, such as Courtright (2007), Agarwal, Xu, and Poo (2009), and particular sections of Case and Given (2016). I call these categories of environment, task, actor, etc., the "elements" of context in Section 3.3.

The "categories or elements" relate to the "facets and types" of context discussed in Section 1.2.1. For example, environment can map to "context as environment or container" or "context as setting"; task/activity/problem/situation can map to "context as situation"; actor can map to "context as the actor's mind"; source/system/channel can map to "context as information horizon"; and time/space can map to "context as time, place, embodiment, and portability." We discuss these further in Section 2.3.

You might also find that some studies are repeated in different sub-sections below. I do this because these studies have investigated the effect of more than one contextual variable on a particular aspect of information behavior. Thus, when discussing a specific variable, it is important not to miss those studies that have looked at this variable (even if we have seen the study previously with respect to another variable in a different sub-section).

Also, throughout the discussion on context variables, there are those variables pertaining, for example, to the actor and the source that are relatively more stable across situations, while others (pertaining, for example, to the task and the situation) are more dynamic/changing, and have a more direct effect at the point of human-information interaction leading to information behavior. It might be useful to distinguish these two types of context variables to understand which variables might only apply in a particular situation, and which might apply across multiple situations. This might also help when choosing research variables when designing research studies incorporating context in information behavior. In the tables in the sub-sections below, where applicable, I mark examples of these relatively more stable context variables in italics. I do not intend this marking of more stable context variables to be exhaustive or authoritative. Rather, my intention is just to provide examples.

a. Type of Information Behavior Studied (dependent variable)

Most of the studies examined the effects of contextual variables on a particular outcome or dependent variable. The contextual variables could be independent (cause in a cause-effect relationship), mediating (something affected by the cause and one that, in turn, leads to the effect) or, sometimes, moderating variables (that affect the relationship between the cause and the effect—see MacKinnon, 2011).

The effect or outcome (dependent variable) was typically a type of information behavior; most studies related to information seeking behavior, and its variants such as source or channel selection for information seeking, or information search and retrieval from a computer system. The categorization of dependent variables here is faceted. Each facet could be affected by particular contextual (independent/mediating/moderating) variables. Representative empirical studies are profiled below that show the effect of contextual variables on each facet or type of dependent variable. Even though some facets such as information seeking behavior, and information search and interaction behavior appear to be similar, they need to be discussed separately as information search and interaction is a specific type of seeking that focuses on computer-based systems as sources for information (Wilson, 1999). Other studies investigated the role of context in other information behavior and practices, such as serendipitous information encountering, collaborative seeking, or knowledge creation. A few studies also looked at dependent variables apart from information behavior—like decision making and learning outcomes, where contextual variables and information behavior impacted that outcome. Even as we discuss the different dependent variables in this section, we are more interested in identifying the contextual factors that affect the particular information behavior, as those variables (either independent, mediating or moderating) are the ones that constitute context which leads to behavior.

Information Seeking Behavior Affected by Context

Studies exploring the role of context for *information seeking* included those by Anderson (2005), Steinerová (2008), Fransson (2012), Mikkonen and Vakkari (2012), Pang (2014), Kekäläinen, Arvola, and Kumpulainen (2014), and Enwald et al. (2015). See Table 2.3 for a summary of key findings from these studies. In the table, I have italicized examples of the relatively stable attributes of context. Hultgren and Limberg (2003) review the literature on the relationships among learning, school assignments, and children's information seeking.

In a longitudinal ethnographic study lasting over two years, Anderson (2005) explored decisions made by two informants involved in scholarly research. The informants used *relevance judgment* and *information seeking* as part of their ongoing research projects. Steinerová (2008) interviewed Ph.D. students to examine what factors impacted their relevance judgments when conducting research, and identified several factors relating to the actor, task, information required, environment, and time. Fransson (2012) found that the navigation strategies used by visitors to a digital library depended on their skill using the Internet, their task, and whether they were interested in browsing or fact-finding. Mikkonen and Vakkari (2012) concluded that public library patrons who read books often were more likely to conduct known-item searching and to browse the shelves; frequent fiction readers were more likely to browse than non-fiction readers. In a Singapore-based study, Pang (2014) saw that during crisis situations, people's age affected their coping style, which in turn affected how frequently they searched for crisis-related information and the sources they chose. Kekäläinen et al. (2014) found that people can find relevant information in a document faster when they are allowed to browse through the document to understand its context. Enwald et al. (2015) deduced that young Finnish men's level of health information literacy and personal health factors affected their preference for positive vs. fear-based health information.

Table 2.3: Contextual variables affecting information seeking behavior		
Context Category	**Context variables identified**	**Source(s)**
Environment	*The collective discourse of the research community*	Steinerová (2008)
Task/situation	Task; browsing or fact-finding	Fransson (2012)
Need/information required	Importance and utility of the information	Steinerová (2008)
Actor	Subjective state of the reader, including mood, knowledge state and impact of previous information seen; information overload; *skill using the Internet; book-reading habits; age; coping style; information literacy*	Steinerová (2008); Fransson (2012); Mikkonen and Vakkari (2012); Pang (2014); Enwald et al. (2015)
Source/system	Location, format, and channel of the information; characteristics of the document itself, such as author and style	Steinerová (2008)
Time/space	Time pressure	Steinerová (2008)

Information Search and Interaction Behavior Affected by Context

Wilson (1999) defines *information searching* as "a subset of information seeking, particularly concerned with the interactions between information user…and computer-based information systems" (p. 263). A related term is *information interaction*—this term may be understood from the description for the IIiX conference, which mentioned exploring "the relationships between the contexts that affect information retrieval [IR] and information seeking, how these contexts impact information behavior, and how knowledge of information contexts and information behaviors can help design truly interactive information systems" (ACM Digital Library, 2017). The conference (now termed CHIIR) draws upon the diverse research communities in information seeking behavior, user interface design for IR systems, and IR system design.

Studies that have looked specifically at *information searching*, *interaction*, and *retrieval* from electronic sources include Liu et al. (2010), Eickhoff, Dekker, and de Vries (2012), Hughes-Morgan and Wilson (2012), MacFarlane et al. (2012), Singer, Norbisrath, and Lewandowski (2012), Brennan, Kelly, and Arguello (2014), Gossen, Höbel, and Nürnberger (2014), Schaller, Harvey, and Elsweiler (2014), Sarrafzadeh et al. (2016), Bailey and Kelly (2016), Edwards and Kelly (2016), and Huurdeman, Wilson, and Kamps (2016). Many of these studies used controlled experiments and were done in a university setting. Table 2.4 summarizes the key findings from these studies. As with the previous tables, I have *italicized* examples of the relatively more stable context variables pertaining to the actor, e.g., age, cognitive abilities, personality, and the more stable source variables e.g., system features. I have also italicized the task stage/phase, because it is part of the larger process, which will have a more immediate actor-information interaction process within it.

Liu et al. (2010) found that online image searchers' "characters" could be categorized along three dimensions: whether their information goal was fixed or evolving, whether their search strategy was cautious or risky, and whether their evaluation threshold was weak or precise. Through an experiment with elementary-school children, Eickhoff, Dekker, and de Vries (2012) concluded that children in higher grades were more likely to be "power searchers." Hughes-Morgan and Wilson (2012) found that interaction method (query suggestion, hierarchical browsing, or faceted filtering) affected participants' number of queries and query refinements made, task completion time, and their perceived ease of use and satisfaction with the system. MacFarlane et al. (2012) saw that dyslexic university students read fewer documents and judged fewer search results as irrelevant when completing a search task. Singer et al. (2012) found that the more complex a search task is, the less accurate people are in estimating the task's difficulty and effort required; they are also less able to judge whether they have correctly completed the task. In Pharo and Nordlie's (2012) study, participants' prior knowledge and task phase affected how many books they examined in a simulated digital bookstore and how many books they judged to be relevant to the task. Brennan et al. (2014) found that participants' cognitive abilities (perceptual speed and visualization abilities) impacted several aspects of search behavior, including number of queries and number of documents viewed, and also affected participants' mental workload. Gossen et al. (2014) conducted an experiment to compare children's and adults' search behavior. The results showed that participants' age affected their search efficiency, search success, and patterns of gaze fixation on the search results page.

In Agarwal (2014), I studied factors that prompt a child between the ages of two and four and a half to engage, disengage, and reengage with touch-based devices (iPhone and iPad). I concluded that the child is able to move seamlessly between the digital and physical environments. Schaller et al. (2014) found that people's needs and priorities for a music festival (e.g., to attend one specific event or to explore all events on a particular bus route) impacted which searching and browsing features they used in an app developed to help people plan their itineraries. In an experiment comparing two search engine interfaces—knowledge graphs and hierarchies—Sarrafzadeh et al. (2016) saw that the participants' prior knowledge of a topic and type of goal in seeking (specific vs. diversive) determined how much time they were willing to spend seeking and which interface they preferred. Bailey and Kelly (2016) developed a model of factors that affect online search expertise, which included prior experience with the topic and system and one's cognitive and affective state. Edwards and Kelly (2016) found that a person's level of interest in a task affected their prediction of task difficulty, time spent on the task, and level of engagement. Huurdeman et al. (2016) applied Kuhlthau's (1991) Information Search Process model to study how search engine use changes at different stages of a task. According to their findings, the use of search engine interface features (query box, search button, filters, saved results), number of queries, words per query, number of pages visited, time spent on a page, gaze fixation, and the perceived usefulness of features changed depending on the task stage.

Table 2.4: Contextual variables affecting information search and interaction behavior

Context category	Context variables identified	Source(s)
Environment	Embodiment, shared context with others	Agarwal (2014)
Task/situation	Task complexity; *task stage/phase*; task ability to engage	Singer et al. (2012); Pharo and Nordlie (2012); Agarwal (2014); Huurdeman et al. (2016)
Need/information required	Type of information goal; need and priority	Liu et al. (2010); Schaller et al. (2014); Sarrafzadeh et al. (2016)
Actor	*Age, grade level*, search expertise, dyslexia, *cognitive abilities (perceptual speed and visualization abilities)*, mental workload, prior topic knowledge, cognitive and affective states, level of interest in task, prediction of task difficulty, *personality, identity, interests, hobbies*, curiosity	Eickhoff, Dekker, and de Vries (2012); MacFarlane et al. (2012); Pharo and Nordlie (2012); Brennan et al. (2014); Agarwal (2014); Gossen et al. (2014); Sarrafzadeh et al. (2016); Bailey and Kelly (2016); Edwards and Kelly (2016)
Source/system	*System features: query suggestion, hierarchical browsing, faceted filtering; device aesthetics*, interactivity, portability, embodiment, variety of apps	Hughes-Morgan and Wilson (2012); Agarwal (2014)
Actor-source relationship	Prior experience with system	Bailey and Kelly (2016)

Source/channel Choice Affected by Context

An information source (e.g., a person, a book, or a search engine) is a repository or carrier that can provide knowledge or information. A channel can be understood as the medium or mode of communication between the source and the actor, e.g., face-to-face, phone, email, text message, etc. (Xu, Tan, and Yang, 2006; Agarwal, 2011). Non-personal channels can include reading a physical book or an electronic book on Kindle, or browsing a website on a computer or smartphone. However, many past studies have used the terms *source* and *channel* synonymously (Agarwal, 2011). Studies exploring the role of context in *source/channel choice* include Byström (1997), Abad-Garcia, Gonzalez-Teruel, and Sanjuan-Nebot (1999), Mackenzie (2005), Bronstein (2010), Bartlett, Ishimura, and Kloda (2011), Agarwal, Xu, and Poo (2011), Saastamoinen, Kumpulainen, and Järvelin (2012), Du, et al. (2013), Kim and Sin (2015), and Sun and Zhang (2016). Table 2.5 summarizes the key findings from these studies, with examples of relatively more stable actor and source/system attributes italicized.

Using a diary study and interviews, Byström (1997) studied how municipal administrators completed work tasks and made decisions. In her study, task type and complexity affected what kind of information the administrators needed, as well as the type and number of sources they consulted. In a study of physicians in a hospital in Spain, Abad-Garcia et al. (1999) found that task type and characteristics of source/channel significantly affected source/channel choice. Mackenzie (2005) investigated how managers choose which coworkers to use as information sources. The most important factors included the coworkers' skills, job roles, and relationship with the information seeker. In Bronstein (2010)'s study, library and information science students identified accessibility to be important for networked sources, and quality and reliability of information provided to be important for human sources. When biologists chose a bioinformatics tool, Bartlett et al. (2011) found system factors (platform, interface, and cost), functionality, customizability, scalability, speed, quality/reliability, usability, learnability, task, familiarity, and the academic background of the user to be important. In my study of knowledge workers in Singapore (Agarwal, Xu, and Poo, 2011), we found that characteristics of the source, task, and the actor-source relationship affected source choice. In Saastamoinen et al.'s (2012) study, city administrators' work roles and prior knowledge of a task affected their perceptions of task complexity, which in turn affected their choice of source and how long they spent searching for information. Du et al. (2013) found the uniqueness of source, appropriateness, familiarity, recommendation from peers, authority, currency, accessibility, and task type to be important in source and channel choices made by marketing professionals. Kim and Sin (2015) deduced that college students' gender, information need, and problem-solving style all had an impact on their choice of social media sites for information seeking, as well as the way they evaluated any information found. Sun and Zhang (2016) found that people with higher information literacy were more likely to use search engines for both factual and exploratory health information seeking, and less likely to use social networking and crowdsourcing sites. People with extroverted personalities were less likely to use search engines to find stories about personal health experiences.

Table 2.5: Contextual variables affecting source/channel choice		
Context category	**Context variables identified**	**Source(s)**
Task/situation	Task type; complexity	Byström (1997); Abad-Garcia et al. (1999); Bartlett et al. (2011); Agarwal, Xu, and Poo (2011); Saastamoinen et al. (2012); Du et al. (2013)
Need/information required	Type of information need	Kim and Sin (2015)
Actor	*Work role*; prior task knowledge; *academic background; gender; problem-solving style; personality type; level of information literacy*	Bartlett et al. (2011); Saastamoinen et al. (2012); Kim and Sin (2015); Sun and Zhang (2016)
Source/system	Accessibility, comfort, speed, *quality/ reliability/ authority/* currency / *appropri-ateness/ job role/ skills*; uniqueness, recom-mendation from peers *System platform, interface, cost*, functionality, *customizability, scalability, speed, quality/ reliability, usability, learnability*	Abad-Garcia et al. (1999); Mackenzie (2005); Bronstein (2010); Bartlett et al. (2011); Agarwal, Xu, and Poo (2011); Du et al. (2013)
Actor-source rela-tionship	Relationship with human source; source/ system familiarity	Mackenzie (2005); Bartlett et al. (2011); Agarwal, Xu, and Poo (2011); Du et al. (2013)

Other Information Behavior and Practices Affected by Context

So far, we have been looking at a specific type of information behavior, and have identified context variables affecting that type of information behavior. While we saw studies investigating informa-tion seeking, information search, and source/channel choice, a number of studies have looked at other behavior within this overall facet or wider umbrella of *information behavior and practices*. Here, information behavior includes encountering, use, sharing (see Wilson, 2010), stopping, creating, collaborative behavior, and other practices.

One of the newer trends in the information science field is the concern with *information practice*, as distinct from information behavior. Savolainen (2008) defines information practice as "a set of socially and culturally established ways to identify, seek, use, and share the information available in various sources such as television, newspapers, and the internet" (p. 2). Cox (2012) calls it "information in social practice." Specifically, practice theory explicitly takes into account the role of context in shaping practices (see Tabak, 2014; Jarrahi and Thomson, 2017). Cox (2012) writes that in information behavior, 'the implicit norm is the individual rational actor actively pursuing a pre-given cognitive need' (p. 9), which "reflects reliance on theory from psychology, rather than from sociology or anthropology" (p. 9). "The logic of practice theories is that what is information is specific to a practice" (Cox, 2012, p. 9). For more depth writings on the concept of information practices, see Schatzki et al. (2001), Savolainen (2007, 2008), and Cox (2012). While Cox (2012) refers to the notion of communities of practice for knowledge sharing in the knowledge management field, practice theory has also been applied to other areas to study the information practices of: patrons and librarians during face-to-face reference interaction in a library (Cavanagh, 2013); people living with chronic health conditions (Lloyd, Bonner, and Dawson-Rose, 2014); transnational migrants as they become familiar with new urban surroundings (Lingel, 2015); and archaeologists, students and volunteers undertaking an excavation in the field (Olsson, 2016).

Table 2.6: Types of information behavior and related contextual variables

Type of Information Behavior Studied	Env.	Task	Need	Actor	Time	Source(s)
Seeking	X	X		X		Algon (1997); Dixon and Banwell (1999); Askola, Atsushi, and Huotari (2010); Gyllstrom and Moens (2012)
Encountering	X			X		Askola, Atsushi, and Huotari (2010); Gyllstrom and Moens (2012)
Use	X	X		X		Algon (1997); Dixon and Banwell (1999)
Sharing		X				Algon (1997)
Stopping	X		X		X	Berryman (2006, 2008); Crescenzi, Kelly, and Azzopardi (2016)
Creating	X					Suorsa and Huotari (2014)
Collaborative behavior	X	X				Bruce et al. (2003)
Metacognitive monitoring					X	Crescenzi, Kelly, and Azzopardi (2016)
Behavior	X	X		X		Allen and Wilson (2003); Ishimura and Bartlett (2013)

In the sections below, we look at the overall facet of information behavior and practices. Table 2.6 lists the different types of information behavior and the contextual variable types that were found to influence these behaviors.

Table 2.7 follows the format of the tables in the previous sections, where I summarize the specific contextual variables identified in the studies. I have italicized examples of the relatively more stable aspects of the environment and task/situation. An actor attribute such as goal/intentionality is closely related to task and is situation-dependent. It is likely to be a dynamic and changing aspect of context. The studies are described below.

Algon (1997) studied individuals working on project teams in a multinational pharmaceutical company to determine the relationship among task assignments, steps and *information-related behaviors* (information *finding*—seeking; information *using*—absorbing, conceptualizing, manipulating, organizing; and information *providing*—providing, verbalizing). Dixon and Banwell (1999) investigated the information seeking and decision-making behaviors of British school governors, and found it affected by individual and organizational variables. Askola, Atsushi, and Huotari (2010) studied the *information practices* (*information seeking vs. information encountering*) of Finnish and Japanese university students in a health information context. Gyllstrom and Moens (2012) analyzed Wikipedia access logs and distinguished two types of users: serendipitous and directed surfers. These two types followed semantically different kinds of links and followed click trails of different lengths.

In a case study of public policy workers in Australia, Berryman (2006, 2008) studied the factors influencing judgements of "enough" information in work-based information seeking. She found the *influences of stakeholders and work colleagues and decision-making style of the employing organizations* to be significant. Apart from environment, other task, need and time/space variables were also important. Crescenzi, Kelly, and Azzopardi (2016) concluded that placing a time limit on searching affected participants' perceptions of task difficulty, satisfaction with the search, their decision to stop searching, and their level of *metacognitive monitoring* (i.e., how closely they kept track of their search progress and the time remaining).

Suorsa and Huotari (2014) found that the knowledge creation process among employees of a children's reading program was shaped by characteristics of the organization, including diversity, flexibility, goals, and the employees' familiarity with each other. Bruce et al. (2003) observed that the collaborative information behavior of design engineers is affected by the nature of the task, as well as the structure and culture of the organization; in addition, even when engaged in a group task, the engineers did not conduct every information activity collaboratively.

Allen and Wilson (2003) studied the role of organizational climate in influencing the degree to which human information behavior moves from being beneficial to the organization to creating overload. Ishimura and Bartlett (2013) studied the differences in research behaviors and information literacy between Canadian and Japanese college students. They found cultural effects on research behavior, as well as effects of prior experience, motivation, and the characteristics of the assignment itself.

Table 2.7: Contextual variables affecting different information behavior and practices		
Context category	**Context variables identified**	**Source(s)**
Environment	*Organizational climate*, influences of stakeholders and work colleagues, decision-making style of the employing organizations, *culture, structure, diversity,* flexibility, *organizational goals*, employees' familiarity with each other, availability of resources, support received	Dixon and Banwell (1999); Allen and Wilson (2003); Bruce et al. (2003); Berryman (2006, 2008); Askola, Atsushi, and Huotari (2010); Ishimura and Bartlett (2013); Suorsa and Huotari (2014)
Task/situation	*Task assignments*, steps, nature, problem dimensions	Algon (1997); Bruce et al. (2003); Berryman (2008); Ishimura and Bartlett (2013)
Need/information required	"Enough" information	Berryman (2006, 2008)
Actor	Goal/intentionality, prior experience, motivation, (evolving) understanding of role/task	Dixon and Banwell (1999); Berryman (2006); Gyllstrom and Moens (2012); Ishimura and Bartlett (2013)
Time/space	Time constraints	Berryman (2006); Crescenzi, Kelly, and Azzopardi (2016)

Other Outcomes Affected by Context

So far, we have looked at studies in which particular types of information behavior were dependent variables affected by context. Studies have also investigated other outcomes apart from information behavior such as *decision making* (Case, 2010) and *learning outcomes* (Collins-Thompson et al., 2016). Here, information seeking/searching strategies are used as independent or mediating variables leading to these outcomes. Barry (1997) reported changes in information behavior, information environment and research activities arising from the use of electronic resources (pre-print bulletin boards and email) for the 48 research projects conducted by the participating physicists. Case (2010) found that coin collectors rely on their prior experience, discussion with other collectors, and various information seeking strategies to reduce their uncertainty and to come to a decision on whether to purchase an item for their collection. Collins-Thompson et al. (2016) explored how Web search strategies affect students' learning outcomes. They found that the number and variety of search queries used affected the participants' time spent reading documents and their cognitive learning scores.

In the sections above, we identified different contextual variables that affect a particular type of information behavior. These variables were grouped into the context categories of environment, task/activity/problem/situation, need/information required, actor, source/system/channel, actor-source relationship, and time/space. In the following sections, we will discuss each of these context categories in greater detail. We will review the literature and identify specific variables belonging to these categories that emerged from prior studies. These variables would be independent (or mediating/moderating) variables in studies of information behavior and practices.

b. Environment

Many studies in information behavior have described context as environment, container, or setting, or all that surrounds the actor in his/her search for information (e.g., Lamb, King, and Kling, 2003; Rieh, 2004; Berryman, 2008; Suorsa and Huotari, 2014). Here, contextual variables could relate to the environment, country, region, setting, space, life world, small world (Chatman, 1991, 1996), group, social network (Shah, 2017), organization, team, workspace, social norms (Chatman, 1996), and the proxy/intermediary/gatekeeper for seeking (Lakshminarayanan, 2010). The environment the actor is surrounded by, and is part of, influences his/her information seeking process and the type of source s/he uses, as well as other information behavior. This environment may be organizational (most often researched, and would typically include a team the actor is a part of), social (including the actor's friends and family in everyday life), cultural or even systemic/technological in nature. Shah (2017) describes how environment could constitute social spaces on the Internet such as Yahoo! Answers, WikiAnswers, and Twitter where people go to seek, acquire and share information. This environmental context (organizational/social/cultural/systemic) has a history and varies with time (Ingwersen and Järvelin, 2005, p. 261).

Courtright (2007) cites studies on environment variables in both workplace and everyday life settings, classifying them under rules and resources, culture (strategies, preferences, and interests), social networks or social capital, social norms or social authority, and collaborative requirement in workplace. Shah (2012) extensively reviews studies on collaboration and collaborative information seeking in the workplace and in everyday life settings. Shah (2017) focuses on social information seeking. Widén and Hansen (2012) report on the effects of organizational information culture on collaboration. In the studies reviewed, the environmental context included characteristics of the organization, social network, culture and physical environment. See Table 2.8. In the table, I have highlighted examples of relatively stable environmental variables across situations in italics. Also see the physical context (Figure 2.11) in Jumisko-Pyykkö and Vainio's (2010) model.

Feng, Apers, and Jonker (2004) categorized environmental context as physical environment (time, location, temperature, humidity, noise, light, vibration, etc.), social environment (traffic jam, surrounding people, etc.), and computational environment (surrounding devices, etc.). According to them, for context-aware computing, a system could gather information on the actor's physical environment from sensors like GPS, on the social environment via service providers, propagated communication, or inferred from user's activity, and on the computational environment by inferring from the user's environment and activity.

Organizational and Social Network—Structure, Goals, Resources, Familiarity, etc.

In an organizational setting, characteristics of the organization and team, including team size, support, and cohesiveness influence the information behavior of the actor. In a study of design engineers, Bruce et al. (2003) found that collaborative information behavior is affected by the nature of the task, as well as the *structure and culture of the organization*. Suorsa and Huotari (2014) saw that the knowledge creation process among employees of a children's reading program was shaped by characteristics of the organization, including *diversity, flexibility, goals*, and the *employees' familiarity with each other*. Among the factors influencing judgements of "enough" information in work-based information seeking by public policy workers, Berryman (2008) found the *influences of stakeholders and work colleagues* and the *decision-making style of the employing organization* to be significant. Along with actor, source, need and time variables, in Steinerová's (2008) study of Ph.D. students to examine what factors impacted their relevance judgments when conducting research, the *collective discourse of the research community* was important.

Culture—Information Culture, Organizational Climate, etc.

Among other actor variables, Dixon and Banwell (1999) found that information behavior of British school governors was affected by the *information culture* and *available resources* of the school, and the *amount of support received* from other governors. In a UK study, Allen and Wilson (2003) concluded that *organizational climate* may play a significant role in influencing the degree to which human information behavior moves from being beneficial to the organization to creating overload. In their case study of a multinational bank, there was a recursive relationship between climate and culture, where a *climate of mistrust* reinforced a *culture of risk avoidance*. Askola, Atsushi, and Huotari (2010) found significant *cultural differences* in the health information environments (types of sources used) and practices (information seeking vs. encountering) between Finnish and Japanese university students. In a study of the differences in the research behaviors and information literacy of Canadian and Japanese college students, Ishimura and Bartlett (2013) observed *cultural effects* on research behavior.

Physical Environment—Embodiment

In my study of a child's use of touch-based devices, *embodiment* (Lakoff and Johnson, 1999; Dourish, 2001) emerged as an important environmental variable, i.e., the ability to place the device in a physical environment, like on a swing in the backyard. The *shared context* of the child with parents and peers to play, communicate and self-express was also important (Agarwal, 2014).

Table 2.8: Environment variables identified in studies on information behavior

Environment Category	Environment Variables Identified	Source(s)
Organization	*Structure*; diversity, flexibility, *goals; organizational decision-making style*; resources, support	Dixon and Banwell (1999); Bruce et al. (2003); Berryman (2008); Suorsa and Huotari (2014)
Social network	Influences of stakeholders and work colleagues; *collective discourse of community*; employees' familiarity with each other; shared context	Berryman (2008); Steinerová (2008); Suorsa and Huotari (2014); Agarwal (2014)
Culture	Information culture; *organizational climate*; cultural differences in information environments and practices; culture	Dixon and Banwell (1999); Allen and Wilson (2003); Askola, Atsushi, and Huotari (2010); Ishimura and Bartlett (2013)
Physical environment	Embodiment	Agarwal (2014)

c. Task/Activity/Problem/Situation

In organizational settings, the need to look for information is often triggered by a project or task. For a student in a university, it could be an assignment given by a professor. In everyday life settings, it could be a situation involving family, friends or one's physical, psychological or financial conditions that triggers a need to look for, find, share, or use information. While *task* is often more applicable to a work or study situation (though there could be personal tasks as well), a generic term that also applies to everyday life could be *activity*—also used by Dourish (2004) (the Sanskrit term *karma* used in literature pertaining to the religions of Hinduism and Buddhism is also a synonym for work or activity). The activity could be understood to be any state ranging from no activity (doing nothing in particular) to intense activity (e.g., running, finishing work before a deadline, etc.).

Thus, contextual variables can concern the situation, problem, task or activity, activating mechanism (Wilson and Walsh, 1996) or trigger (Karunakaran et al., 2013). Vakkari (1999), Kim and Allen (2002), Byström and Hansen (2005), and Courtright (2007) cite a number of empirical studies that support the premise that user's search performance and/or patterns differ depending on the task. Variables of a work task situation can include requests for information, pressures and constraints (cost, time), domains, goals, information preferences, strategies, etc. The task or problem situation can vary based on type, specificity, domain, stage, complexity, importance, engagement, or interdependency. See Table 2.9. I have italicized examples of relatively stable aspects of task across different situations.

Nature, Goal, Dimension, Characteristic

Researchers have classified the type, nature, dimensions, characteristics, and goal of tasks in different ways. Byström (1997) found that task type (automatic information processing, normal information processing, normal decision, and known-genuine decision) and complexity affected what kind of information administrators needed, as well as the type and number of sources they consulted. In the Human-Computer and Information Retrieval (HCIR) community, there are many attempts to distinguish the work task from the seeking/search task. For example, Borlund (2003) provided suggestions for developing simulated work task situations as stimuli for studies of searching behaviors. Byström and Hansen (2005) also identified two different levels of a work task—information seeking tasks, and information search—each affected by other contextual factors. Thus, a work task can have different seeking sub-tasks, with each seeking sub-task having one or several search and retrieval sub-tasks. Much of the review below would apply to seeking and search tasks, within a larger work task. Matthews, Lawrence, and Ferguson (1983) compared subject and known-item searches. In a study to determine the relationship among task assignments, steps, and information-related behaviors, Algon (1997) classified tasks as interacting with others, interacting with ideas or information, and interacting with things, and further divided them into subcategories (pp. 214, 217). Spool et al. (1999) defined four types of questions: simple fact questions, judgment questions, comparison of fact questions, and comparison of judgment questions. Kim (2000) classified tasks as topical vs. factual. Bhavani, Drabenstott, and Radev (2001) proposed a taxonomy of tasks derived from analyzing 100 email requests. They classified them based on what the user knows vs. what s/he requires from the search. In an experiment with university students and faculty, Liu et al. (2010) categorized online searchers' information goals as fixed or evolving.

Specificity

Researchers have also classified tasks by degree of specificity. Saracevic and Kantor (1988) found that the specificity and complexity of a search task have an impact on search behavior. Marchionini (1989) investigated closed and open tasks. Qiu (1993) looked at general vs. specific tasks. Pfaffenberger (1996) divided tasks based on the amount of information needed for a topic into three types of questions: finding specific information, collecting a few sources of high quality information, and collecting everything exhaustively on a topic. Sarrafzadeh et al. (2016) found that the type of goal in seeking (specific vs. diversive) determined how much time undergraduates were willing to spend seeking and which of two search interfaces they preferred. In Kiseleva et al.'s (2016) study, factors affecting user satisfaction with intelligent assistants like Siri and Alexa included type (simple vs. mission) and complexity of the task.

Domain, Topic, Type

Studies have looked at the role of the domain or topic of the task in information behavior, e.g., a task related to business, finance, medicine, law, etc., or some specific aspect of any of these or other topics. Taylor (1991) developed the Information Use Environment (IUE) framework that "looks at the [actor] and the uses of information and the contexts within which those [actors] make choices about what information is useful to them at particular times" (Taylor, 1991, p. 218). IUE's basic analytical framework includes four components: people, setting, problems, and problem resolutions. Taylor examined it for engineers, legislators and physicians, and the problems or work tasks they engaged in. In the studies below, we look at the role of domain, topic or type in affecting behavior. I list studies investigating mostly work tasks (Byström and Hansen, 2005) below, with studies like Fransson (2012) being an example of seeking/search tasks. Abad-Garcia, Gonzalez-Teruel, and Sanjuan-Nebot (1999) found *task type* to significantly affect source/channel choice. *Job and task type* affected the type of information need, which, in turn, affected the urgency of search. Bruce et al. (2003) found that collaborative information behavior of design engineers is affected by the nature of the task. Anderson (2005) concluded that focusing on scholarly researchers' ultimate *research goals* rather than on *retrieval tasks* provides a fuller understanding of the relationship between goals and their articulation in interactions with information systems. In her case study of how public policy workers judge when they have "enough" information, Berryman (2006, 2008) found work-ers' (evolving) understanding of the task and *problem dimensions* to be among the relevant factors. In Bronstein's (2010) study of the choice of sources/channels by library and information science students, task types were seen to be important. In Bartlett, Ishimura, and Kloda's (2011) study of factors affecting the choice of bioinformatics tool, the *user's task* was one of the relevant factors. Fransson (2012) found that users' navigation strategies in a digital library depended on their search task, and whether they were interested in browsing or fact-finding. In Ishimura and Bartlett's (2013) study of differences in the research behaviors and information literacy of Canadian and Japanese college students, the characteristics of the school assignment affected research behaviors.

Stage, Step, Phase

Studies have also found the stage, step, or phase of a task to affect information behavior. Kuhlthau's (1991) model describes the actors' feelings, thoughts and behaviors during different phases of infor-mation search process. Pharo and Nordlie (2012) deduced that the task phase affected how many books in a simulated digital bookstore the participants examined and how many books they judged to be relevant to the task. Huurdeman, Wilson, and Kamps (2016) applied Kuhlthau's (1991) model to study how search engine use changes at different stages of a task. They found that *task stage* im-pacts many search behaviors of computer science students, including the use of different interface features, the number and length of queries, the number of pages visited, and the location of gaze fixation on the search page.

Complexity, Difficulty, Uncertainty, Non-routineness, Intellectual Demand

Researchers have also frequently investigated the effect of complexity or difficulty of a task or problem situation on information behavior (e.g., as I did in Agarwal, Xu, and Poo, 2011). Wildemuth, Freund, and Toms (2014) review the interactive information retrieval literature on task complexity. They seek to disambiguate task complexity from task difficulty and identify both as multidimensional constructs. They identified six task attributes to operationalize search task complexity—number of subtasks or steps; number of subtopics or facets; number of query terms and operators required; number of sources or items required; the indeterminate nature of the task; and the cognitive complexity of addressing the information need. For search task difficulty, they identified four attributes—actor's search performance; actor's perceptions of difficulty; the match between terms in the task description and in the target page; and the number of relevant documents in the collection. The first two attributes for task difficulty are both subjective variables (Wildemuth, Freund, and Toms, 2014).

Other related variables include uncertainty (O'Reilly, 1982; Culnan, 1985; Byström and Järvelin, 1995; Byström, 2002), non-routineness (Lawrence and Lorsch, 1967), and intellectual demand (Gray and Meister, 2004). Singer, Norbisrath, and Lewandowski (2012) found that the more complex a search task is, the less accurate people are in estimating the task's difficulty and effort required; they are also less able to judge whether they have correctly completed the task. In Saastamoinen, Kumpulainen, and Järvelin's (2012) study, the administrators' work role and prior knowledge of a task affected their perceptions of task complexity, which in turn affected their choice of source and how long they spent searching for information. Crescenzi, Kelly, and Azzopardi (2016) found placing a time limit on searching affected participants' perceptions of task difficulty. Edwards and Kelly (2016) saw that undergraduate students' level of interest in a task affected their prediction of task difficulty, time spent on the task, and level of engagement.

Importance, Urgency

Importance is another pertinent task variable (Xu, Tan, and Yang, 2006). In Agarwal, Xu, and Poo (2011), my colleagues and I investigated the effect of task importance, task urgency and task complexity on the source choice behavior of knowledge workers in Singapore.

Interdependency, Engagement

Tasks can also vary based on interdependency (Campion, Medsker, and Higgs, 1993). Tasks outside of work tasks (e.g., an activity in everyday life information seeking) can also vary depending on the degree of engagement they provide. In my study of a child's use of touch-based devices, the tasks or activities varied based on their ability to engage vs. to provide sustained engagement, e.g., watching videos and solving puzzles vs. clicking a picture (Agarwal, 2014).

Task/Activity/ Problem/ Situation Category	Task/Activity/ Problem/Situation Variables Identified	Source(s)
Type	Type, nature, goal, dimension, characteristic	
	• *Work task, seeking task, searching task*	Byström and Hansen (2005)
	• Automatic information processing, normal information processing, normal decision, and known-genuine decision	Byström (1997)
	• *Subject and known-item searches*	Matthews et al. (1983)
	• Interacting with others, interacting with ideas or information, and interacting with things	Algon (1997)
	• *Simple fact questions, judgment questions, comparison of fact questions, and comparison of judgment questions*	Spool et al. (1999)
	• *Topical and factual*	Kim (2000)
	• What the actor knows vs. what s/he needs from search	Bhavani et al. (2001)
	• Fixed or evolving information goal	Liu et al. (2010)
Specificity	• Specific vs. general	Saracevic and Kantor (1988); Qiu (1993)
	• *Closed vs. open*	Marchionini (1989)
	• Finding specific information, collecting a few sources of high-quality information, and collecting everything exhaustively	Pfaffenberger (1996)
	• Specific vs. diversive goal	Sarrafzadeh et al. (2016)
	• Simple vs. mission	Kiseleva et al. (2016)

Table 2.9: Task/activity/problem/situation variables identified in studies on information behavior

Domain	Domain/topic/context specific	Abad-Garcia et al. (1999); Bruce et al. (2003); Anderson (2005); Berryman (2008); Bronstein (2010); Bartlett et al. (2011); Fransson (2012); Ishimura and Bartlett (2013)
Stage	*Step, phase*	Kuhlthau (1991); Algon (1997); Pharo and Nordlie (2012); Huurdeman et al. (2016)
Complexity	Complexity, difficulty, uncertainty, non-routineness, intellectual demand	Lawrence and Lorsch (1967); O'Reilly (1982); Culnan (1985); Saracevic and Kantor (1988); Byström and Järvelin (1995); Byström (1997, 2002); Gray and Meister (2004); Agarwal, Xu, and Poo (2011); Singer et al. (2012); Saastamoinen et al. (2012); Wildemuth, Freund, and Toms (2014); Crescenzi et al. (2016); Edwards and Kelly (2016); Kiseleva et al. (2016)
Importance, urgency		Xu, Tan, and Yang (2006); Agarwal, Xu, and Poo (2011)
Interdependency		Campion et al. (1993)
Engagement	Level of engagement provided	Agarwal (2014)

d. Need/Information Required

Information need has been at the heart of information science and information behavior research for several decades now, dating back to Wilson's, Dervin's and Belkin's work in the early 1980s, and even earlier if we consider Taylor's (1968) typology. The field of information behavior was earlier termed Information Needs, Seeking and Use (INSU). Information need can be characterized in various ways (see Cole, 2012; Case and Given, 2016; Agarwal, 2015; Line, 1974).

Need—Trigger

The difficulty with understanding need is that it resides inside the actor's head, and yet doesn't always originate from within the actor. Often, the need arises within the actor as a result of his/her/their interaction with the environment. Wilson (1981) wrote that the term information need might be misleading. It is better understood as information required or sought in response to or toward the satisfaction of some need—which might be psychological, intellectual, physiological, emotional, etc.

In everyday life, Savolainen (2012) examined the literature on the contexts in which information need arises. Apart from need arising in the actor's mind as a result of the actor's cognitive or affective state (thoughts or feelings—the internal context), which he leaves out, Savolainen found three commonly discussed triggers for information need. The trigger could be: (1) a situation—variables in time and space, e.g., in everyday life, some external object or interaction might pique one's curiosity, leading to a need to look up something on Google or to ask a friend; (2) a work task or problem solving; or (3) a discourse—conversation with other people. These are three different ways of understanding need, but they are not mutually exclusive. You can have situational factors within a task, and conversation that happens during a task or problem solving. The problem situation, task or discourse gives rise to an information need, which resides in the mind of the actor and keeps changing, constant only at a specific point in time and space. This need plays a vital role in the specific knowledge required and sought by the actor. See Taylor (1968), Line (1974), Case and Given (2016, pp. 79-91), Cole (2012), and Agarwal (2015) for a fuller discussion on information need.

Need—Task-based

Morrison (1993) classified information needs as task mastery information needs, role clarification information needs, acculturation information needs or social integration information needs. Of these, task problem solving is the most common information need (Gerstberger and Allen, 1968; O'Reilly, 1982; Yitzhaki and Hammershlag, 2004; Xu, Tan, and Yang, 2006; Agarwal, Xu, and Poo, 2011). Abad-Garcia, Gonzalez-Teruel, and Sanjuan-Nebot (1999) found *information need of physicians* to be a mediating variable, where job and task type affected the type of information need, which, in turn, affected the urgency of search.

Need—Everyday Life

Everyday life needs (Savolainen, 1995) might arise as an interaction of the actor and his/her/their environment and could be of emotional or entertainment value. Questions like "why is the sink clogged?" or "should I bring my umbrella with me today?" or "is recycling collection this week or next week?" might form part of the actor's everyday information need. Schaller, Harvey, and Elsweiler (2014) developed an app to help people plan their itineraries during a music festival. They found that people's needs and priorities for the festival (e.g., to attend one specific event or to explore all events on a particular bus route) impacted which searching and browsing features they used in the app. Kim and Sin (2015) examined how social media sites are used by college students for information seeking. In their study, the respondents' information need had an impact on their choice of social media sites for information seeking, as well as the way they evaluated any information found.

Need—Changing Nature

Because information need resides within the actor's mind, it is hard to study, and hard to comprehend from a system designer's point of view. A person creating the software for a search engine or information retrieval system has to grapple with this need in the actor's head, which might have arisen from the interaction of a number of contextual factors such as actor, situation, task, or discourse. Using Savolainen's (2012) classification of triggers for information need (where he leaves out the actor's mind) would somewhat help limit the scope of an actor's information need from a designer's point of view.

In addition, information need is not fixed. Every answer returned by a search engine might satisfy or not satisfy the actor's need in one or more ways, and the actor might initiate a new search on the basis of a new need. In collaborative information behavior (where two people are working together physically, or connecting remotely with each other on a shared screen), a conversation with or a remark from one's colleague might change the nature or extent of one's individual information need, as well as the collective need of the collaborating team. In synthesizing studies related to serendipity in information behavior, I distinguished between current and different information need (Agarwal, 2015). Here, current need is based on the task at hand or the actor's curiosity, while different information need is one that arose in a different context than the current one. I would map current need to Taylor (1968)'s conscious need, and different need to visceral need in Taylor's classification.

Information Required—Tacitness, Observability, Systemic Nature

When a situation, task or discourse gives rise to an information need in the mind of the actor, the actor approaches an information source to find information to help address the need. The required information may vary depending on its degree of tacitness (Polanyi, 1967), observability, and its systemic nature (Roberts and Deitrich, 1999, p. 984), which affects the difficulty or cost of acquiring it. Tacitness implies information that is difficult to put into words (we know much more than we can tell). The more tacit the information is, the less communicable it is. Observability means how easy or difficult it is for others to observe what one is doing and the information therein. The professional autonomy, secrecy, and monopoly in workplaces make a lot of information difficult to observe (Roberts and Deitrich, 1999). Systemic nature is the extent to which an element of information is independent or part of a system. Roberts and Deitrich relate it to professional services such as medicine, or when expert advice is sought. All of these can directly or indirectly contribute to the degree of complexity of the information required. The complexity of the information required is often related to the task complexity, which we discussed in the previous section.

Information Required—Judgements of Enough, Importance, Utility

A related concept is satisficing (Simon, 1956), or the act of deciding when you have enough information to meet a need. In a case study of public policy workers, Berryman (2008) studied factors influencing judgements of *"enough" information*. Another variable is the importance of the information needed. Through interviews of Ph.D. students, Steinerová (2008) found that the importance and utility of the information impacted their relevance judgments when conducting research.

Table 2.10 lists examples of studies based on different dimensions of information need and information required by the actor. I do not mark any specific variables as relatively stable here, as information need is likely to change in time and space (though a specific need for information could be part of a more stable need based on job and task type, or based on everyday life).

Table 2.10: Variables of need and information required identified in studies on information behavior

Need Category	Need Variables Identified	Source(s)
Information need	Trigger, changing nature	Taylor (1968); Line (1974); Cole (2012); Agarwal (2015)
	Based on job and task type	Gerstberger and Allen (1968); O'Reilly (1982); Abad-Garcia et al. (1999); Yitzhaki and Hammershlag (2004); Xu, Tan, and Yang (2006); Agarwal, Xu, and Poo, (2011); Kim and Sin (2015)
	Based on everyday life	Savolainen (1995); Schaller et al. (2014); Kim and Sin (2015)
Information required	Judgments of "enough"	Berryman (2008)
	Importance and utility	Steinerová (2008)
	Tacitness	Polanyi (1967)
	Observability	Roberts and Deitrich (1999)
	Systemic nature	Roberts and Deitrich (1999)

e. Actor

A unit of analysis is what or whom you study in your research. In the field of knowledge management, this would typically be an organization or a project within that organization. In computer science, it would be a system, a piece of software, lines of code, or a procedure. In information science and information behavior research, the unit of analysis is most often the actor, the person, the individual in question, the seeker, or the user. This is because we are concerned with the motivations, journey and success of the actor in the process of needing, finding and sharing information. At times, the unit could consist of a team or group.

The actor (persons, seekers, or users as a category) is not a monolith, but is rather one's own individual. Dervin describes the actor as a "body-mind-heart-spirit moving through time and space, with a past history, present reality and future dreams or ambitions" (Foreman-Wernet, 2003, p. 7). While people might share some similarities based on gender, culture, education, value system, experience, etc., the combination of all these factors always creates a unique person at a given point in time—something that is very often overlooked as we seek to fit people within "buckets" of our choosing, a process termed stereotyping in social science research (Tajfel and Turner, 1979; also see Agarwal, 2009a).

Context variables relating to the actor include the relatively stable attributes such as demographic variables—age, gender, nationality, education, etc., personality, cognitive style, habits, disabilities, work role or domain, etc. NAIS (2017) provides a sample of actor variables (which they refer to as sample culture identifiers). The sample includes ability, age, ethnicity, gender, race, religion, sexual orientation, socioeconomic status (class), body image ("lookism"), educational background, academic/social achievement, family of origin, family make up, geographic/regional background, language, learning style, beliefs (political, social, religious), and globalism/internationalism. They have moved away from an earlier listing of "big 8" or "core identifiers"—(1) ability—mental and/or physical; (2) age; (3) ethnicity; (4) gender; (5) race; (6) religion; (7) sexual orientation; and (8) socio-economic status/class)—because "they implied a sense of hierarchy, placing greater value on the identifiers in the list over other identifiers" (NAIS, 2017).

The actor also has attributes that change more often depending on the situation such as prior knowledge, goals, affective/emotional state, psychological state, skills (if they can change pretty readily), and motivation. Studies on information avoidance have also looked at actor variables such as the desire to avoid information or to ignore information need, which might change depending on the situation. In Table 2.11, I summarize the actor variables found in studies of information behavior. I have italicized examples of relatively stable actor attributes across different situations.

Feng, Apers, and Jonker (2004) categorized user-centric (or actor-centric) context as background (interest, habit, preference, working area, subjective opinion, etc.), dynamic behavior (intention, task, activity, etc.), physiological state (body temperature, heart rate, etc.) and emotional state (happiness, sadness, disgust, fear, anger, surprise, calmness, etc.). According to them, for context-aware computing, a system could gather the background information from the actor's profile, the dynamic behavior from the actor's agenda, the physiological state from body sensors, and emotional state via a multimodal analysis of the actor's visual and acoustical features.

We discuss the relatively stable actor attributes below.

Demographics

A number of studies have found actor demographic variables to be important. Bartlett, Ishimura, and Kloda (2011) saw academic background to be relevant to the choice of a bioinformatics tool. Eickhoff, Dekker, and de Vries (2012) found that children in higher grades were more likely to be "power searchers". In Gossen, Höbel, and Nürnberger's (2014) study, participants' age affected their search efficiency, search success, and patterns of gaze fixation on the search results page. Pang (2014) found that people's age affected their coping style, which in turn affected how frequently they searched for crisis-related information and the sources they chose. Kim and Sin (2015) observed that college students' gender and problem-solving style had an impact on their choice of social media sites for information seeking, as well as the way they evaluated any information found.

Personality

Individual personality and the actor's cognitive style also play an important role in information behavior. These individual differences include the actor's problem-solving style (Wu, Custer, and Dyrenfurth, 1996), cognitive abilities (Allen, 2000; Brennan, Kelly, and Arguello, 2014), and cognitive style (Ford and Chen, 2000; Wang, Hawk, and Tenopir, 2000). Brennan et al. (2014) found that participants' cognitive abilities such as perceptual speed and visualization abilities impacted several aspects of search behavior, including number of queries and number of documents viewed, and also affected participants' mental workload. In my study of a child's use of touch-based devices, the actor variables that prompted the child to engage, disengage, and reengage were the child in context, and personal unique attributes based on personality—"it's mine!", identity (Agarwal, 2009a), interests, hobbies, curiosity, and age (Agarwal, 2014). Crescenzi, Kelly, and Azzopardi (2016) found that placing a time limit on searching affected their satisfaction with the search and their level of *metacognitive monitoring* (i.e., how closely they kept track of their search progress and the time remaining).

Habits

The actor's habits and behavior also affect his/her/their information behavior practices and preferences. Bronstein (2010) found students' habits to be an important variable in her study of their choice of sources/channels. Mikkonen and Vakkari (2012) concluded that people who read books often are more likely to conduct known-item searching and to browse the shelves in a public library; frequent fiction readers were more likely to browse than non-fiction readers.

Disability

The presence of a disability can also affect search behavior. MacFarlane et al. (2012) found that dyslexic university students read fewer documents and judged fewer search results as irrelevant when completing a search task.

Work role

We also discussed Work roles in Section 2.2.1 Populations studied (Table 2.1). A number of studies have found work role or domain to be important. Dixon and Banwell (1999) saw that information behavior of British school governors was affected by the individual's understanding of the role and his/her personal experience. In Saastamoinen, Kumpulainen, and Järvelin's (2012) study, administrators' work role and prior knowledge of a task affected their perceptions of task complexity, which in turn affected their choice of source and how long they spent searching for information. See Courtright (2007) and Case and Given (2016, pp. 278–319) for more examples of studies on work domain or role, as well as human activity. Case and Given (2016) review the occupational categories of scientists and engineers, social scientists, humanities scholars, health care providers, managers, journalists, lawyers, farmers, and other occupations. They also review studies based on the actor's social role, such as citizen or voter, consumer, hobbyist, gatekeeper, patient, student, and so on (pp. 319–345). Other related variables are tenure in position and tenure in organization. Experienced employees seek less knowledge since they know much of what is needed to perform well (Tesluk and Jacobs, 1998; Gray and Meister, 2004; Agarwal, Xu, and Poo, 2011).

Actor variables that may change more readily depending on situation are discussed below. The assumption below is that the actor is learning rapidly, which leads to a change in prior knowledge and skills. Mood and motivation is likely to change more often.

Prior Knowledge

Prior domain knowledge or background knowledge plays a role because most seekers come with insufficient background knowledge (Miller and Jablin, 1991; VandeWalle et al., 2000; Kwasitsu, 2003; Case, 2010; Pharo and Nordlie, 2012; Sarrafzadeh et al., 2016). While the level of domain knowledge might affect the amount of information sought, because an expert might consider it less profitable to ask other people compared to a novice, it is unclear how domain knowledge alters the source choice (or use) criteria (Xu, Tan, and Yang, 2006). Anderson (2005) explored decisions made by two informants involved in scholarly research. The actor variables explored in the study included the informants' prior knowledge and understanding. Steinerová (2008) examined what factors impacted Ph.D. students' relevance judgments when conducting research. She found the subjective state of the reader, including knowledge state and impact of previous information seen, as well as information overload to be important. In a study of the differences in the research behaviors and information literacy of Canadian and Japanese college students, Ishimura and Bartlett (2013) observed effects of prior experience and motivation on research behaviors. In Enwald et al.'s (2015) study, young Finnish men's level of health information literacy and personal health factors affected their preference of positive vs. fear-based health information. Bailey and Kelly (2016) found that librarians' prior experience with the topic and system affected their online search expertise. Sun and Zhang (2016) concluded that people with higher information literacy were more likely to use search engines for both factual and exploratory health information seeking, and less likely to use social networking and crowdsourcing sites.

Skills

One's skills and experience with the search system, tool or device also affect search behavior. Borgman (1989) examined individual differences in information retrieval in terms of personal characteristics, technical aptitudes, and academic orientation and concluded that these factors were interrelated. Fransson (2012) found that users' navigation strategies in a digital library depended on their skill using the Internet.

Affective State

Apart from prior knowledge, the subconscious fears, experiences, biases and impulses of the actor also affect information behavior. These are things that the actor may not be fully cognizant of, and may form part of the actor's peripheral awareness. They can be likened to the visceral, subconscious need in Taylor's (1968) typology of information need. In his book, *Predictably Irrational*, Dan Ariely (2008) alludes to these "hidden forces" that shape our behavior and decisions, which he says are "systematic and predictable." The affective state of the actor, including mood and emotion, information overload and attitude toward risk, is also important to information seeking behavior (Nahl and Bilal, 2007; Steinerová, 2008; Eickhoff et al., 2012; Liu et al., 2014; Bailey and Kelly, 2016). Fourie and Julien (2014) review literature on emotion in information behavior. Savolainen (2016) describes affective barriers to information seeking.

Motivation

Interest and the degree to which the actor is motivated play an important role in the frequency and choice of sources for information seeking. Dispositional factors such as learning orientation (Gray and Meister, 2004; Agarwal, Xu, and Poo, 2011), and need for achievement (Morrison and Vancouver, 2000) determine the level of intrinsic motivation a seeker has and can impact his/her usage of an information source. Gray and Meister (2004) also studied two other dispositional variables, risk aversion and reciprocation wariness. Risk-averse individuals might source more knowledge as a way of reducing the possibility of making an error. Reciprocation-wary individuals might source less knowledge for fear of being exploited in an exchange relationship (Gray and Meister, 2004). Borlund, Dreier, and Byström (2012) found that a person's interest in the topic affects the amount of time spent on a search.

Table 2.11: Actor variables identified in studies on information behavior

Actor Category	Actor Variables Identified	Source(s)
Demographics	*Academic background; age; gender*	Bartlett et al. (2011); Eickhoff et al. (2012); Gossen et al. (2014); Pang (2014); Agarwal (2014); Kim and Sin (2015)
Personality	*Coping style; cognitive ability/ style; perceptual speed; visualization abilities; personality—"it's mine!", extroversion; identity; problem-solving style; metacognitive monitoring; risk aversion; reciprocation wariness*	Borgman (1989); Wu et al. (1996); Allen (2000); Ford and Chen (2000); Wang et al. (2000); Gray and Meister (2004); Agarwal (2009a); Pang (2014); Brennan et al. (2014); Agarwal (2014); Kim and Sin (2015); Crescenzi et al. (2016); Sun and Zhang (2016)
Habit	*Habits; reading habits; hobbies*	Bronstein (2010); Mikkonen and Vakkari (2012); Agarwal (2014)
Disability	*Dyslexia*	MacFarlane et al. (2012)
Work role	*Work domain; work role; tenure in position; tenure in organization; social role*	Tesluk and Jacobs (1998); Dixon and Banwell (1999); Gray and Meister (2004); Agarwal, Xu, and Poo (2011); Saastamoinen et al. (2012); Courtright (2007); Case and Given (2016)
Prior knowledge	Experience, domain knowledge, knowledge state, impact of previous information seen, understanding; pre-search confidence; information literacy; cognitive state	Miller and Jablin (1991); Dixon and Banwell (1999); VandeWalle et al. (2000); Kwasitsu (2003); Anderson (2005); Xu et al. (2006); Steinerová (2008); Case (2010); Pharo and Nordlie (2012); Saastamoinen et al. (2012); Ishimura and Bartlett (2013); Enwald et al. (2015); Bailey and Kelly (2016); Sarrafzadeh et al. (2016); Sun and Zhang (2016)
Skills	Search skills; prior experience with system; technical aptitude	Borgman (1989); Fransson (2012); Bailey and Kelly (2016)

Affective state	mood; information overload; attitude toward task; affective state	Nahl and Bilal (2007); Steinerová (2008); Eickhoff et al. (2012); Liu et al. (2014); Bailey and Kelly (2016)
Motivation	interest; motivation; curiosity; academic orientation; learning orientation; need for achievement	Borgman (1989); Morrison and Vancouver (2000); Gray and Meister (2004); Agarwal, Xu, and Poo (2011); Borlund et al. (2012); Ishimura and Bartlett (2013); Agarwal (2014)

f. Source/System/Channel

Christensen and Bailey (1997) define *information source* as a repository that can provide knowledge or information. Xu, Tan, and Yang (2006) define sources as carriers of information. Xu, Tan and Yang (2006), and my colleagues and I (Agarwal, Xu, and Poo, 2011; Agarwal, 2011) differentiate between an information source, information content and a channel. The same content or information can be available from multiple sources, and a specific source can provide different types of information. One source can also be better at providing one type of content compared to another type.

Table 2.12 lists the contextual variables associated with sources or channels in studies on source/channel use, choice, or preference. These include quality, accessibility and source type (Xu, Tan, and Yang, 2006; Agarwal, Xu, and Poo, 2011). Also refer to the technical and information context (Figure 2.11) in Jumisko-Pyykkö and Vainio's (2010) model, and other studies on context-aware computing (mentioned in Section 2.2.4). In the table, examples of source/system variables that are likely to change more frequently depending on situation are appropriateness, usefulness, customizability, place, and physical proximity. A source could vary by situation, e.g., through personalization or because a personal source is taking a certain role that is situation-specific. Other source/system variables may be relatively stable, and are italicized in Table 2.12.

Quality and Accessibility

Source quality refers to the benefit provided by an information source and can be defined as the novelty, reliability, and relevant scope of information content the source carries for the task at hand (Xu and Chen, 2006). In our survey of 352 knowledge workers, my colleagues and I (Agarwal, Xu, and Poo, 2011) also studied other source variables that represent the cost associated with using an information source. *Accessibility* is the time and effort required and the difficulty associated with reaching a source, which might be both physical and mental. Communication difficulty and understandability are the difficulties associated in communicating with the source once the seeker has reached the source or is able to access it (Agarwal, Xu, and Poo, 2011).

A number of studies have looked at the impact of source quality and accessibility on source choice. Abad-Garcia, Gonzalez-Teruel, and Sanjuan-Nebot (1999) found that task type and characteristics of source/channel, including accessibility, speed, appropriateness and comfort, significantly affect source/channel choice. Bronstein's (2010) study of library and information science students regarding their choice of sources/channels, found the physical proximity of a source, its ease of use, quality, and currency to be important. Du et al. (2013) investigated marketing professionals' source and channel choices. A source's uniqueness, appropriateness, authority, and currency all affected the participants' choice, as well as their familiarity with the source and recommendations from peers.

Type, Dimension

The *type* of source might be [inter]personal (friends, colleagues, etc.) or impersonal (books, online sources, etc.) (Agarwal, Xu, and Poo, 2011). In Agarwal, Xu, and Poo, we posit that "when a seeker makes a source choice decision, the channel decision is often implicitly made" (p. 1088). We identify two dimensions of channels—physical-electronic and synchronous-asynchronous. In Agarwal (2011), I classify types of sources (incorporating channels) into one of five types—face-to-face, phone/online chat, email/online forums, book/manual and online information. In Agarwal, Xu, Lawrence, and Agarwal (2012), we study four types of access channel—laptop, desktop, smartphone, and tablet—which vary by degree of portability of the device.

Human sources. Studies have also focused exclusively on human sources. For example, Mackenzie (2005) investigated how managers choose which coworkers to use as information sources and found the coworkers' skills and job roles to be important.

Books and electronic sources. Some studies have looked at library books and electronic resources. In a two-year qualitative study of theoretical physicists, Barry (1997) reported on the impact of the *use of electronic resources* (pre-print bulletin boards and email) on information behavior, environment and research activities for the 48 research projects conducted by the participants during that period. Steinerová (2008) interviewed Ph.D. students to examine what factors impacted their relevance judgments when conducting research. She found the place, format and channel of the information, and the characteristics of the document itself, such as author and style to be important.

Systems and technology. While the variables applying to sources and channels would apply to system sources as well, there are other variables that pertain only to systems and technology. These might consist of systemic and interactive features and information objects that deal with knowledge representation, thesaural nets and content/structures. Interfaces have functions with interactive features. The information technology (IT) components consist of retrieval engines, database architecture, indexing algorithms and computational logics (Ingwersen and Järvelin, 2005). Other variables associated with impersonal sources include perceived usefulness and perceived ease of use of a system or technology (Davis, 1989).

Bartlett, Ishimura, and Kloda (2011) found system factors like interface, cost, customizability, and functionality to be relevant to researchers' choice of a bioinformatics tool. In Hughes-Morgan and Wilson's (2012) study, the search interaction method—query suggestion, hierarchical browsing, and faceted filtering—affected participants' number of queries and query refinements made, task completion time, and their perceived ease of use and satisfaction with the system. In my study of a child's use of touch-based devices, the source/system variables that prompted the child to engage, disengage, and reengage were device aesthetics, interactivity, portability, embodiment, and variety of apps (Agarwal, 2014). Kiseleva et al. (2016) studied what factors led to user satisfaction with intelligent assistants like Siri and Alexa. They found that these factors included the quality of the voice recognition function. Sarrafzadeh et al. (2016) compared two search interfaces—knowledge graphs and hierarchies—in an experiment with undergraduate students. According to their findings, knowledge graphs reduced the number of documents that needed to be read to complete a task.

Table 2.12: Source/system/channel variables identified in studies on information behavior

Source/System/Channel Category	Source/System/Channel Variables Identified	Source(s)
Type	*Interpersonal vs. impersonal; dimension*	Agarwal (2011); Agarwal et al. (2011)
Quality	*Quality; authority;* appropriateness; *uniqueness; people – skills, job roles; reliability;* usefulness; *documents—author, style; currency; system—interface,* customizability, *functionality, features, interactivity, search interaction method, information objects; device—aesthetics; apps—variety*	Davis (1989); Abad-Garcia et al. (1999); Mackenzie (2005); Ingwersen and Järvelin (2005); Xu and Chen (2006); Xu et al. (2006); Steinerová (2008); Bronstein (2010); Agarwal et al. (2011); Bartlett et al. (2011); Hughes-Morgan and Wilson (2012); Du et al. (2013); Agarwal (2014); Kiseleva et al. (2016); Sarrafzadeh et al. (2016)
Accessibility	*Accessibility, speed, place, format,* physical proximity, *impersonal—ease of use; cost; communication difficulty; understandability; device—portability, embodiment*	Davis (1989); Barry (1997); Abad-Garcia et al. (1999); Xu et al. (2006); Steinerová (2008); Bronstein (2010); Agarwal et al. (2011); Bartlett et al. (2011); Agarwal et al. (2012); Agarwal (2014)

g. Actor-source Relationship

The degree of success in the process of information seeking depends to a large extent on the relationship shared by the actor and the source, i.e., the cost incurred by the actor in getting the information out of the source. Table 2.13 lists the actor-source relationship variables identified in studies on information behavior. These variables are more likely to be situation-dependent and are not italicized in the table.

Social Risk, Comfort

For human or interpersonal sources, a number of studies have found the actor-source relationship to be important (e.g., Ashford, 1986; Miller and Jablin, 1991; Pettigrew, Fidel, and Bruce, 2001; Agarwal, Xu, and Poo, 2011). There can be different aspects to this relationship such as social risk, e.g., embarrassment, loss of face, revelation of incompetence (Ashford, 1986); or social benefit, e.g., relationship building, making an impression; and other variables, such as degree of comfort (Abad-Garcia et al., 1999; Agarwal, Xu, and Poo, 2011), willingness to share and level of closeness. Vancouver and Morrison (1995) found that source expertise, accessibility, *relationship quality*, and reward power significantly affected whether undergraduate students chose to seek feedback from sources or not. In Abad-Garcia, Gonzalez-Teruel, and Sanjuan-Nebot's (1999) study, task type and characteristics of source/channel and *comfort with the source* significantly affected source/channel choice. Mackenzie (2005) investigated how managers choose which coworkers to use as information sources. She found the coworkers' *relationship with the information seeker* to be the most important.

Expectation

Anderson (2005) studied the informants' *expectations about source* in an ethnographic study of scholar researchers. In Agarwal and Rahim (2014), we analyzed data on expectations from a cross-cultural virtual collaboration by students based in the U.S. and Singapore.

Familiarity

Familiarity with the source or system is another important factor. In a study of factors affecting the choice of bioinformatics tool, Bartlett, Ishimura, and Kloda (2011) found the *user's familiarity with the system* to be one of the relevant factors. Du et al. (2013) found that marketing professionals' familiarity with the source and recommendations from peers affected their source and channel choices. Suorsa and Huotari (2014) studied knowledge creation among employees of a children's reading program. Among other factors, the knowledge creation process was shaped by the employees' familiarity with each other.

For impersonal sources such as library or search engines, related factors of the actor-source relationship can be ease of information extraction, comfort level in using the system, etc. The searcher's system-knowledge, namely the searcher's familiarity or expertise with the information system and searching techniques, will also determine his/her level of comfort in using an impersonal source such as an online search engine or a knowledge repository.

Table 2.13: Actor-source relationship variables identified in studies on information behavior

Relationship Category	Actor-source Relationship Variables Identified	Source(s)
Social risk	Embarrassment, loss of face, revelation of incompetence	Ashford (1986)
Comfort	Degree of comfort, quality	Vancouver and Morrison (1995); Abad-Garcia et al. (1999); Mackenzie (2005); Agarwal et al. (2011)
Expectation		Anderson (2005); Agarwal and Rahim (2014)
Familiarity	Degree of familiarity with source/system	Bartlett et al. (2011); Du et al. (2013); Suorsa and Huotari (2014)

h. Time/Space

There is a context associated with the actual interaction (or session) between the actor and the source during the process of information seeking or other information behavior. Variables such as time of interaction, place of interaction and the history of past interaction all have a bearing upon information behavior (also see Ingwersen and Järvelin, 2005, Chap. 6). Dervin calls it space-time in her Sense-Making Methodology central metaphor (Dervin and Foreman-Wernet, 2012).

Time and space provide for the immediacy of the actor's environment when interacting with information. The fact that an actor can see snow outside, get diverted for a while on Facebook, pet a dog or cat sitting nearby, hear a television switched on in the next room, or be aware of a colleague working nearby are all parts of the actor's environment in time and space that influence the actor's information behavior process.

Time Constraint, Time Limit, Time Pressure, Spatial Location, etc.

Researchers have studied time in different ways. Berryman (2006) interviewed public policy workers to learn how they decided when to stop a search for information. One of the reasons for search stopping included *time constraints*. Steinerová (2008) found time pressure and information overload important in her study of Ph.D. students to examine what factors impacted their relevance judgments when conducting research. Borlund, Dreier, and Byström (2012) examined what affects the amount of time people spend on a search. Important factors included a person's interest in the topic, the difficulty of the search, and the amount of relevant information available. Liu et al. (2014) found that placing a time constraint on a search task affects searchers' pre-search confidence, their estimate of the time needed to complete the task, their mood, and their perception of knowledge gained. Crescenzi, Kelly, and Azzopardi (2016) found that *placing a time limit on searching* affected participants' perceptions of task difficulty, satisfaction with the search, their decision to stop search-ing, and their level of metacognitive monitoring.

Jumisko-Pyykkö and Vainio's (2010) model (Figure 2.11) incorporates temporal context, which lists duration, time of day/week/year, before-during-after, actions in relation to time, and synchronicism (synchronous vs. asynchronous) as sub-components, which also could be variables or measures studied in relation to time. The sub-components in Jumisko-Pyykkö and Vainio's such as spatial location, functional place and space, artifacts, etc. would map to space.

2.2.4 APPLICATION OF CONTEXT IN SYSTEM DESIGN

We had earlier discussed information search and interaction behavior affected by context in the be-ginning part of Section 2.2.3 when discussing type of information behavior as a dependent variable in prior research studies. I have included this separate section because the design of information search and retrieval systems is a major field where the knowledge of the user's context becomes very important. Allen (1996) also wrote on the need for user-centered information-system design. Apart from studies in information seeking and behavior that focus on the user, a number of re-search articles in information retrieval, focusing on system and technology, have reported progress in incorporating context into system design—in personalizing search systems and improving the relevance of search results for the actor. Jumisko-Pyykkö and Vainio (2010) look at the components and sub-components of context (which would map to some of the variables we looked at in the pre-ceding sections), and arrive at a model of context for use in human mobile system interaction (Fig-ure 2.11). From a system design perspective, Hinze and Buchanan (2005) categorized context into network context, device context, and application context, with the actor or user context being part of the application context. The attempt to create systems that deduce the actor's context has played a central role in the related areas of human-computer interaction, such as ubiquitous computing (Weiser, 1999), context-aware computing (Dey, Abowd, and Salber, 2001), pervasive computing (Ark and Selker, 1999), embodied interaction (Dourish, 2001, 2004), and computer-supported cooperative work.

Dourish (2004) has been a major influence on the application of context in information interaction and retrieval. He talks about two views of context: positivist and phenomenological. He terms the positivist view as concerned with the problem of encoding and representing context, and uses prior definitions to highlight four assumptions in the positivist view—that context is a form of information, that context is delineable, that context is stable, and that context and activity are separable.

In taking a stand that context is an interactional rather than a representational problem, he describes the situation, which he terms awkward, of trying to derive positivist responses to phenomenological and sociological arguments—the critique being that "the kind of thing that can be modeled, … [using the assumptions of the positivist view] …, is not the kind of thing that context is" (Dourish, 2004, p. 22). Dourish argues that contextuality is a relational property in respect to two things, e.g., the actor and the system or the actor and the environment (as opposed to an inherent property of a single entity); context is defined dynamically (as opposed to being something that can be delineated and defined in advance); context is an occasioned property (like ordinariness defined by Sacks, 1984), relevant to particular settings, instances of action or doing in a given moment, and parties to that action (as opposed to something that is stable); context arises from the activity—activity produced, maintained, and enacted in the course of the task at hand (as opposed to being just "there," and separable from content, or the actor or the task). Thus, context here is not a stable description of a setting in which the activity or situation arises. It is something that people do, and arises from and is sustained by the activity itself. It is not a premise, but an outcome. It is something that people work on and achieve, rather than simply observe as being there (Dourish, 2004).

Jumisko-Pyykkö and Vainio (2010), Bauer, Newman, and Keintz (2014), and Bauer and Dey (2016) provide examples of incorporating context from the point of view of the system during the system design process, and for context-aware computing and context-aware mobile system design. We had discussed Jumisko-Pyykkö and Vainio (2010) in detail in Section 2.1 Models and frameworks incorporating context.

Studies have reported on approaches to personalize search systems by incorporating the actor's context. Limbu et al. (2006) devised an approach to improve contextual relevance feedback by collecting users' search history and other data, and then using that data to modify search queries and retrieve personalized search results. Smyth (2006) discussed the development of personalized web search and the Collaborative Web Search approach, which learns from the behavior of a specialized community of searchers (e.g., car enthusiasts).

Gyllstrom, Soules, and Veitch's (2008) confluence system kept track of a user's actions relating to specific files in order to identify contextual inter-file relationships to aid in retrieval. Ruthven (2008) discussed the changes in information retrieval system design over time due to the influence of contextual IS&R research, as well as the challenges raised in interface design. Golovchinsky, Diriye, and Dunnigan (2012) developed a system called Querium that supported multi-session exploratory searching by remembering and visualizing retrieval history and incorporating a "like" feature, as well as a variety of query types and result views. Lee, Shah, and Yoon (2014) proposed a system that would create a visualization of a user's knowledge schema by analyzing his/her current information collection. The user could then utilize that visualization to specify his/her information needs and organize new information. Dehghani et al. (2016) developed a method to improve group-based system customization (e.g., for social networks or target demographics) by removing features unique to individual users and finding the abstract model representing the whole group.

Researchers have also tried to improve search relevance for the actor by incorporating context. Daoud, Tamine-Lechani, and Boughanem (2008) built a system that detects the boundaries of a user's search session, and then ranks the search results according to the user's short-term interest. Sondhi, Chandrasekar, and Rounthwaite (2010) proposed a method for creating topical search systems by collecting contextual keywords from topic-specific query logs, and then automatically adding such keywords to topical searches. Lioma, Larsen, and Ingwersen (2012) showed that retrieval performance could be improved using polyrepresentation, or the combination of multiple object representations of e.g., user context, the information sought, and the retrieval system. Researchers have also carried out studies on location-awareness in mobile devices. For example, Galeana-Zapién, Torres-Huitzil, and Rubio-Loyola (2014) proposed an architecture and method for continuous location tracking of the actor based on dynamic context changes. Chen and Jones (2014) built a prototype desktop search system for personal files that allows searching and browsing using episodic contextual metadata associated with a file, e.g., the time of day it was created, the weather at the time, the names of people associated with each file, etc. Tran et al. (2016) proposed a ranking method that uses activity logs and semantic information about personal documents to group the documents according to a user's tasks, allowing for easier retrieval.

2.3   MAPPING THEORETICAL CONCEPTIONS TO ONE CONTEXTUAL ELEMENT

In order to understand how the theoretical conceptions of Chapter 1 can map to the different contextual elements we examined in this chapter, such as the actor, task, source, etc., we can try to identify one element that each theoretical conception best relates to. While it is likely that each conception will relate to multiple elements (e.g., interaction may relate to time/space, actor, source/ system/channel, actor-source relationship, environment, etc.), I list one that has the most direct correlation to the theoretical conception to aid in understanding.

While environment, container, setting, life world/information world, and information ground can be mapped to the actor's environment, role and the actor's mind relate to the actor; situation can relate to task/activity/problem/situation; information horizon/field and pathways can be mapped to source/system/channel; common ground, ordinariness and discourse can be mapped to the actor-source relationship; interaction, time, place, embodiment, and portability can relate to time/space; and constraints (and also relevance, proximity, legacy, and determinant) can be mapped to more than one aspect of context, such as the actor, the environment, the task, etc.

A particular theoretical conception, e.g., context as life/information world, or context as information horizon/field and pathways, can relate to one, more than one, or all aspects of context. In order to be useful, a particular conception need not relate to all aspects or all possible variables of context. This is because each theoretical lens provides a unique perspective on looking at a research phenomenon. The same phenomenon could be viewed from different perspectives to gain different understanding, and to triangulate findings from different viewpoints.

Between 15 and 20 years ago, there were calls by Dervin (1997), Cool (2001), and others to investigate context more holistically. In-context research was formally established with the first Information Seeking Behavior in Context (ISIC) conference in 1996 (Fidel, 2012, p. 145). Despite the seemingly widespread and growing attention, the concept remains ill-defined and inconsistently applied (Cool, 2001). Most literature on information needs, seeking and use fails to address the problem of context theoretically (Dervin, 1997; Johnson, 2003; Lueg, 2002; Courtright, 2007).

Nick Belkin asked in his panel at the First International Symposium on Information Interaction in Context in 2006, "What aspects of your concept of context are essential, important, interesting and necessary for understanding and supporting human interaction with information?" (Ingwersen, Ruthven, and Belkin, 2007). In the last two decades, in-context research has attracted the attention of researchers from fields other than library and information science (LIS), such as information retrieval (IR) and human-computer interaction (Fidel, 2012). Fidel (2012) points out that the elements that are considered in each research project draw de facto the boundaries of its context. She laments that if each study of a phenomenon examines a different context, the findings are ad-hoc and incompatible, and cannot be aggregated into a coherent cumulative body of research that may lead to generalizations.

As Fidel said five years ago, even though a large portion of the scholarly work in information behavior today is in-context research, the community is still discussing the definition of context, and that most empirical research has overlooked this debate (Fidel, 2012). This holds true even today. Despite the need, there isn't any agreement in defining: (1) What does context really mean? How do we map the conceptual space of context? (2) What are the boundaries of context? (3) What are the variables that make up context in information behavior and that can be incorporated into research studies? (4) How can we design research studies incorporating context? (5) How do the boundaries of context move and reshape? and (6) How do we move toward a unified definition of context in information behavior?

2.4   CHAPTER SUMMARY

In this chapter, we reviewed the literature to investigate the role of context in information behavior. Through models and frameworks that have incorporated context, we looked at several classical studies in information behavior. We then examined various empirical studies on information seeking and other forms of information behavior where context has played an important part. The dependent variables that researchers have studied include one or more types of information behavior, and in some cases, application and outcome of this behavior to decision making and learning outcomes. The contextual variables studied include aspects of the environment, the task/problem/situation, the need or information required, the actor, the source/system/channel, the actor-source relationship, and time/space. We also looked at the different populations studied, as well as the research methods used. Finally, we briefly looked at studies that have applied context in system design for information search and retrieval. A review of the literature was important in order to see the work that researchers have done in the area of context as it pertains to information behavior, especially in the last decade.

In the next chapter, we begin the process of addressing the first three questions identified above. Questions 4 and 5 are addressed in Chapters 4. In Chapter 5, we will answer Question 6 and arrive at a definition.

CHAPTER 3

Mapping the Conceptual Space of Context

What we have seen so far in the preceding two chapters is getting a sense of the field—the differing conceptual understandings of context, the contextual elements identified in the many empirical studies on context in information behavior, and how the two can relate to each other. From this chapter onwards, I begin to put forth my own thinking on what context is, as it relates to information behavior. We will address the research questions that we raised at the end of the last chapter. This chapter will address: What does context really mean? How do we map the conceptual space of context? What are the boundaries of context? What are the variables that make up context in information behavior and that can be incorporated into research studies?

We delineate the boundaries of context through the Contextual Identity Framework—where I bring together three views of context—the personal view, the shared view, and the stereotyped view. Each view has three levels—the individual level; the in-group or interpersonal level; and the in-group/out-group or intergroup level. Next, we identity the elements of context through the seven categories of environment, task/activity/problem/situation, need/information required, actor, source/system/channel, actor-source relationship, and time/space. Then we place these context elements within each of the three levels of the three views of the Contextual Identity Framework. Finally, we identify variables within each of these context elements that can be measured in research studies.

3.1   BACKGROUND

3.1.1   SO, WHAT DOES CONTEXT REALLY MEAN? HOW DO WE MAP THE CONCEPTUAL SPACE OF CONTEXT?

a.   Salient Points from Prior Definitions of Context

As I introduced in Chapter 1, many studies have looked at context as something that surrounds the actor—an environment or setting where the actor is situated. This setting is either broad (a country, political environment, company, or organization one is part of) or narrow (one's room at home or an office cubicle). Dourish (2004) terms this the positivist view of context. Within this larger setting is a situation in time and place that is the immediate context for the actor's need for information, the seeking behavior, or another form of information behavior. For example, say you need to book tickets for a vacation. This need to buy tickets is within a larger setting of a country or home, but may be influenced by a conversation with a spouse or friend, as well as other factors such as an upcoming long weekend, and how much control you (or another actor) have over other areas of your life and work. Actor variables such as work role (or a social role) are also context. While the vacation may be a choice, the long weekend is a situation that simply happened (thrownness as described by Heidegger—Dahlstrom, 2013). Even within the choice of vacation, the high price of tickets due to the long weekend is a situation that might *happen* to the actor without much of a choice.

Opposing the positivist view of context as a setting, other researchers have looked at context as the cognitive-affective facets of the actor—the physical state, thoughts, recent experiences, attitude, feelings, fears, etc. that occur in the actor's mind. Thus, the actor might contemplate whether to go on the vacation or not; if yes, where to go, and what mode of transportation to take. These decisions might be informed by the range of information sources that the actor consults. Here, the information horizon (Sonnenwald, 1999; Agarwal, Xu, and Poo, 2011) or field and pathways (Johnson et al., 2006) of the actor is the context. If the actor does decide on this, the situation (another point in time and space within the larger context of the decision to travel and the context of the long weekend) might change to packing and deciding on what to pack. The environment, the situation (thrownness), the actor's own cognitive or affective state, the social circle, and information horizon which affects the information the actor gets all create constraints for the actor. Thus, constraints are also considered context.

Dourish (2004) and Cook (2010) focus on context as assigned meanings during interaction, typically with an electronic device (e.g., the actor's interaction with one's phone when trying to look for ticket options for the vacation), where factors such as relevance, proximity (Lee, 2011; Traxler, 2011), and temporal and spatial aspects become important. With the ubiquity of smartphones, and the actor's ability to carry a phone anywhere, situatedness, embodiment, and portability are important factors when considering context. Here, context becomes "overlapping and fragmentary." (Traxler, 2011, p. 6). Abowd et al. (1999), and Dey (2001) define context as any information that can be used to characterize the situation of an entity, where an entity can be a person, place, or physical or computational object that is considered relevant to the interaction between a user (actor) and an application, including the user and application themselves. Zimmermann, Lorenz, and Oppermann (2007) extend this definition to state that "elements for the description of this context information fall into five categories: individuality, activity, location, time, and relations. The activity predominantly determines the relevancy of context elements in specific situations, and the location and time primarily drive the creation of relations between entities and enable the exchange of context information among entities" (p. 559).

Courtright (2007) reviews the literature on context classified along social, relational and dynamic lines. Her typology includes "context as container," "context as constructed meaning—

person as context," and "socially constructed context: the social actor." The first one would map to Dourish (2004)'s positivist view. Dervin describes this line of thinking as "virtually anything that is not defined as the phenomenon of interest…a kind of container in which the phenomenon resides" (1997, p. 14). The second and the third phrases from Courtright's typology would be closer to his phenomenological view of context, where context is relative and is "created" by the actor at a point in time and space—the point of interaction. Courtright also lists studies proposing that context is relational and embedded within other contexts, and that context is dynamic and changing.

Dourish (2004) criticizes the positivist view of "context as container," listing assumptions it makes about context—that context is a form of information, that it is delineable, that it is stable, and that it is separable from the task or activity at hand. Instead, he posits that contextuality is a relational property, the scope of contextual features is defined dynamically, context is an occasioned property at a given time and space, and that it arises from the activity—it "isn't just 'there', but is actively produced, maintained, and enacted in the course of the activity at hand" (p. 22).

b.   My Stand on the Role and Meaning of Context

So, the question is, does the context create the situation in which the actor engages in information behavior, or does the actor "produce" the context at the point of interaction as Dourish writes? I'd say, "both!" The situation that the actor finds oneself "thrown" in is produced by the context, and the actor, in turn, has leverage to act upon and influence his/her/their context at a point in time and space, and subsequently, in the short- and long-term periods following that time. It is a push and pull that is continuously negotiated. As Ingwersen and Järvelin (2005) write, "actors and other components function as context to one another in the interaction processes" (p. 19).

Let us explore further whether the boundaries of context can be delineated, and if so, how.

3.2   DELINEATING THE BOUNDARIES OF CONTEXT: CONTEXTUAL IDENTITY FRAMEWORK

3.2.1   THE SCOPE OF CONTEXT

Prior research has shown some attempts at setting the boundary of what is and what is not context. Lee (2011), in his definition, tries to separate the actor from the context when he defines context as a "set of things, factors, elements and attributes that are related to a target entity in important ways (e.g., conceptually or pragmatically) but are not so closely related to the target entity that they are considered to be exclusively part of the target entity itself" (p. 96). Callon and Law (1989) write that the boundary between the content (in our case, the actor) and context is pragmatic, permeable, and revisable. Lea, O'Shea, and Fung (1995) describe this boundary as one that is continually negotiated and re-negotiated. Jumisko-Pyykkö and Vainio (2010) list properties to underline the dynamism between the modular descriptions of context. These properties range from macro vs. micro, static vs. dynamic, rhythmic pattern vs. random, etc. The things that remain mostly constant over time (e.g., one's office space, time of browsing, etc.) are static, while things that change, e.g., the webpage one is reading, is dynamic.

As Dourish (2004) suggests, context is of the actor engaged in an activity at the point of interaction. In the case of information behavior, the context of interest is the context of a human-information interaction. This interaction can be conceptualized as an actor conducting some type of interaction with information provided by a source through a channel. In the tables of Section 2.2.3 (and in Table 3.4 that we will see in Section 3.4), when identifying contextual variables pertaining to different elements of context, I have italicized examples of relatively stable attributes of the actor, source/system/channel and other elements. These would be relatively "static" (as per Jumisko-Pyykkö and Vainio, 2010), while the attributes not italicized are more dynamic and likely to change across situations.

It is arguable whether attributes of the source and the actor are part of the context. One could argue that they are the focal point and that their enduring attributes are "not" part of the context; and that context should be construed as including only those elements that surround the interaction, the actor, and the source/system/channel. Those elements may include attributes of the actor and the source/system/channel that are situation-dependent. For example, an actor's interest in the information need or motivation to pursue the information need are dependent on the need and its role in the actor's life world; therefore, they might be included within a conceptualization of the context of the actor addressing the information need. However, attributes like the actor's age, general cognitive style, and personality could be seen as stable attributes of the actor and not part of the context of the interaction of interest. Such an argument would be similar to Lee (2011)'s position whereby if everything of interest is included as part of context, then context cannot be distinguished from the interaction itself. As per Lee (2011), definition, the italicized variables pertaining to the actor, would not be a part of the context.

However, as per Callon and Law's (1989) and Lea, O'Shea, and Fung's (1995) writings, the boundary is permeable and revisable, and one that is continually negotiated and renegotiated. I adopt the latter statements to posit that the individual researcher may decide whether to include those relatively stable attributes as part of context or not. Quantitative studies can include them as control variables to see if they have any effect on the dependent variable, i.e., a type of information behavior. Determining which variable is stable and which is dynamic is also a subjective exercise. This is the reason why I have listed all possible variables relating to the different context elements in the tables in Section 2.2.3 (even while italicizing what I thought were more stable actor and source/system/channel attributes).

3.2.2   THE CONTEXT BEHIND MY STUDY OF CONTEXT

Drawing from my work in Agarwal, Xu, and Poo (2009), I seek to delineate the boundary of context. When I started investigating context more than a decade ago in 2006, most articles I came across looked at context as a container or environment. Christina Courtright (2007)'s review for the now-discontinued *Annual Review of Information Science and Technology* (*ARIST*) on context was extremely helpful. As discussed in Section 3.1, she summarized the empirical studies on context as falling under one of three categories: "context as container," "context as constructed meaning—person as context," and "socially constructed context: the social actor."

Studying context as the container or environment is a convenient and practical approach, and the most prevalent. The view of context as the container was criticized by Dervin (1997), Dourish (2004) and others as being "not real" and positivist—context, they said, is subjective and cannot be just something that surrounds the actor. We can try and understand context as container by comparing it with categorizing and classification that we do in our daily lives, and that we see as necessary as helpful. Units such as seconds, minutes, hours, days, weeks, months and years help us to simplify and abstract, and enable us to make sense of time. The study of the organization of information is core to the practice of library and information science. However, categorizing and classification do not reflect reality. There are countless colors, even though only a small number is used commonly in language. Moments and instances of time are artificially classified as years, months, days, hours, minutes, etc. to help in interpersonal communication. Similarly, context as container or environment, while being convenient and perhaps, necessary, does not reflect reality. As the Nobel prize winning Daniel Kahneman writes when describing intuitive heuristics, "when faced with a difficult question, we often answer an easier one instead, usually without noticing the substitution" (Kahneman, 2011, p. 12). When faced with the difficulty of understanding the full nuances of a person's context when engaged in information behavior, we tend to substitute it with the easier answer of a container or environment surrounding the actor.

Courtright's second view of context was 'context as constructed meaning—person as context' (Dervin, 1997), which is closer to Dourish's (2004) phenomenological view. Even though the chair I'm sitting on while writing is outside of me and independent, what is important is how I feel sitting on it and what I think of it. Often, what I describe of the chair—"Oh! I love this chair" is what I think of the chair, as opposed to what the chair actually is. A statement such as "this snow is awful" or "the snow is beautiful" might be more a reflection of the actor and the actor's mind, as opposed to an attribute of the snow itself. The third view of the "socially constructed context: the social actor" also stems from the phenomenological view and conceptualizes context as influenced by the people we live or work amongst and interact with (as Savolainen, 2012, described when he talked about the context for information need arising during dialog).

The question that took me a month of thinking to figure out was which of these conceptualizations was correct, and which was flawed. Were those researchers who claimed context to be the container or surrounding (something that is external) correct, or were those who claimed context to be a part of me, in my head, and informed by my social connections? The moment of epiphany was realizing that all three were valid views or perspectives on context, and what one concluded to be context depended on the view one was using to envision context. All views were true and co-existed, and were a part of the concept of context. They were just different ways of looking at the same thing. Depending on where you looked at it from, and what you focused on, you would see different things.

The poem "The Blind Men and the Elephant" by John Godfrey Saxe, who lived from 1816–1887, is helpful in illustrating this. This poem was published in Holton and Curry (1914, pp. 107-109). It was adapted from a parable that originated on the Indian subcontinent and that people have widely interpreted and cited in different religious traditions and scientific domains.

Figure 3.1: The blind men and the elephant (Illustration by Maud Hunt Squire in Holton and Curry, 1914, p. 108; via Wikimedia Commons).

It was six wise men of Indostan
To learning much inclined,
Who went to see the Elephant—(though all of them were blind),
That each by observation—might satisfy his mind.

The First approached the Elephant,
And happening to fall
Against his broad and sturdy side—At once began to bawl:
"God bless me! But the Elephant—Is very like a wall!

The Second, feeling of the tusk,
Cried, "Ho! What have we here?
So very round and smooth and sharp—To me 'tis mighty clear
This wonder of an Elephant—Is very like a spear.

The Third approached the animal,
And happening to take
The squirming trunk within his hands,—Thus boldly up and spake:
"I see," quote he, "the Elephant—Is very like a snake!"

The Fourth reached out an eager hand,
And felt about the knee:
"What most the wondrous beast is like
Is very plain," quoth he;
"Tis clear enough the Elephant
Is very like a tree!"

The Fifth who chanced to touch the ear,
Said: "Even the blindest man
Can tell what this resembles most;—Deny the fact who can,
This marvel of an Elephant—Is very like a fan!"

The Sixth no sooner had begun
About the beast to grope,
Than seizing on the swinging tail –That fell within his scope,
"I see", said he, "the Elephant—Is very like a rope!

> *And so these men of Indostan*
> *Disputed loud and long,*
> *Each in his own opinion —Exceeding stiff and strong*
> *Though each was partly in the right —And all were in the wrong!*

The comparison of context to an elephant is, perhaps, not too far off the mark. I used this metaphor of partial views of the elephant to denote the partial views of context, as I conceptualized and worked on the cover painting of this book. Two decades ago, Dervin (1997) titled her paper, "Given a context by any other name: Methodological tools for taming the unruly beast." An elephant has its "broad and sturdy side," the tusk, the "squirming trunk," the leg, the ear, the "swinging tail," and all are parts of the elephant and different ways of looking at it; similarly, the three views of context listed by Courtright (2007) are all different ways of looking at and understanding context. Like the blind men, we might criticize them as positivist (Dourish, 2004) or phenomenological views, but they all belong to the "unruly beast" we know as context. As Werner Heisenberg (1958) wrote, "…we have to remember that what we observe is not nature in itself, but nature exposed to our method of questioning" (p. 57).

Not just different views of context, we saw in Section 2.2.3 that the classification of specific types of information behavior is also faceted, where any of the facets (information seeking, information searching, etc.) could be affected by the different contextual variables (task complexity, actor motivation, etc.), which may belong to particular categories or elements of context (task, actor, environment, etc.). Thus, even particular contextual variables (or groups of variables belonging to particular context elements) investigated in studies are like blind men seeing only a particular aspect/ perspective of the wider phenomenon of the way humans interact with information. Applying one or more variables in investigating the effect of context on information behavior will only measure the effect of a small aspect of the reality of context on behavior, and not of the entire context (even though studies might claim to have studied the effect of context on information behavior).

Let us now look at the theory that further informed my attempt at delineating the boundary of context.

3.2.3   THEORETICAL LENS—SOCIAL IDENTITY THEORY

According to sociological theories of identity by Henri Tajfel and John Turner (1979), the groups people belong to provide them with an important source of pride and self-esteem. Social identity consists of "those aspects of an individual's self-image that derive from the social categories to which he [or she/they] perceives himself as belonging". Social identity "may be positive or negative according to the evaluations of those groups that contribute to an individual's social identity" (p. 40). Tajfel and Turner conceptualize a group as "a collection of individuals who perceive themselves to be members of the same social category, share some emotional involvement in the common definition of themselves, and achieve some degree of social consensus about the evaluation of their group and of their membership in it" (p. 40). Gender, age, education, nationality, religion, region, country of origin, race, ethnicity, etc. are some of the ways in which people see themselves as part of a group (in-group) or distinguish themselves from other groups (out-group).

"The major characteristic of social behavior related to [the] belief system of [stereotyping in in-group/out-group differentiation] is that, in the relevant intergroup situations, individuals will not interact as individuals, on the basis of their individual characteristics or interpersonal relationships, but as members of their groups standing in certain defined relationships to members of other groups" (Tajfel and Turner, 1979, p. 35). Tajfel and Turner distinguished between interpersonal behavior (we can also call it in-group, where you see the other person as part of your group) and intergroup behavior (which we can call in-group/out-group, where you distinguish between those in your group and those outside of it). In the extreme of fully interpersonal behavior, "interactions between two or more individuals …is *fully* [emphasis original] determined by their interpersonal relationships and individual characteristics, and not at all affected by various social groups or categories to which they respectively belong," e.g., relations between spouses, or between old friends. On the other extreme of this continuum, i.e., fully intergroup behavior, "interactions between two or more individuals (or groups of individuals)… are *fully* [emphasis original] determined by their respective memberships in various social groups or categories, and not at all affected by the inter-individual personal relationships between the people involved," e.g., "behavior at a negotiating table of members representing two parties in an intense intergroup conflict" (p. 34). I've tried to summarize this in Figure 3.2. We can understand this as the act of stereotyping. In the figure, the circles surrounding the persons represent the social groups or categories that each of them is a part of.

Interpersonal (in-group)   Intergroup (in-group/out-group)

Figure 3.2: Stereotyping.

Thus, we as humans often tend to stereotype other people (Agarwal, 2009b), and yet see ourselves with complex identities. To provide the example of myself (with multiple, simultaneous identities as everyone has), I can say that I am a male, I am a researcher, I am a professor, I am from this region, I have these hobbies, I have these beliefs, etc. However, whether I immediately recognize all the multiple identities in a person I meet or fall prey to stereotyping based on my limited interaction and one of two aspects of that person's identity is subject to question. We also have shared identities as members of different groups, which we view as nuanced and complex to a certain degree (in-group behavior). By contrast, we might consider people whom we stereotype not to be complex at all, and think we know or understand them, simplifying all of their complexities based on one aspect of their identity, such as race, ethnicity, skin color, gender, nationality, profession, religion, or a one-time interaction (in-group/out-group behavior). As Rabindranath Tagore wrote in his essay "East and West" in the collection, *Creative Unity* (Tagore, 1922):

> *"We are in haste to seek for general types and overlook individuals.*
>
> *When we fall into the habit of neglecting to use the understanding that comes of sympathy in our travels, our knowledge of foreign people grows insensitive, and therefore easily becomes both unjust and cruel in its character, and also selfish and contemptuous in its application...*
>
> *It has been admitted that the dealings between different races of men [humans] are not merely between individuals; that our mutual understanding is either aided, or else obstructed, by the general emanations forming the social atmosphere. These emanations are our collective ideas and collective feelings, generated according to special historical circumstances" (p. 93).*

Citing examples, Tagore goes on to explain that "people have a certain collective idea [of people based on race, ethnicity, skin color, gender, nationality, profession, religion, etc.] that obscures their humanity" (p. 94). "When we approach …[a person] who is under the influence of this collective idea, he is no longer a pure individual with his conscience fully awake to the judging of the value of a human being. He is more or less a passive medium for giving expression to the sentiment of a whole community [or another collective idea based on race, gender, skin color, etc.]" (pp. 93-94). "It is evident that the ..[collective]-idea is not creative; it is merely institutional. It adjusts human beings according to some mechanical arrangement. It emphasises the negative side of the individual—his separateness. It hurts the complete truth in man" (Tagore, 1922, p. 94). Here, Tagore is alluding to the intergroup behavior that people often exhibit, which he says emphasizes separateness (in-group/out-group differentiation), as opposed to interpersonal behavior, where a person is judged by one's individual merit, and not merely by virtue of belonging to some social group.

3.2.4   CONTEXTUAL IDENTITY FRAMEWORK

Drawing from the social identity theory (Tajfel and Turner, 1979), I propose the *Contextual Identity Framework* to explain the different views of context. I first called it Contextual Identity Framework in Agarwal, Xu, and Poo (2009), as the framework is based on the social identity theory and helps explain context. The term "identity" is included because who is viewing the context is an important determinant in how we understand context.

The framework itself can be seen from three views—(1) the personal view of context (the "I" in context, i.e., the actor's context as the actor sees it) (Figure 3.3); (2) the shared view of context (the "we" in context, i.e., a team or a group's context as members of the group see it) (Figure 3.4); and (3) the stereotyped view of context (the "he/she/they" in context, i.e., the context of a person or a group as seen by a person outside the actor's shared context, such as a positivist researcher or a system developer) (Figure 3.5). All the views, in totality, help us understand context. All the views co-exist, are part of the concept of context, and influence each other. They each provide different ways of looking at and understanding context.

a.   **The Personal View of Context**

Figure 3.3 shows the personal view of the Contextual Identity Framework. At the center is the actor engaged in an activity. This includes the actor in time and space, with thoughts, feelings, and moods, attitudes and intelligence, with a sense of history and movement, and other various attributes, including physical, cognitive, affective and psychological (see Dervin, as cited in Foreman-Wernet, 2003; Agarwal, 2012). The IB in the figure indicates a specific information behavior in time and space, such as information seeking, sharing, using, avoiding, finding by chance, etc., and could also be inactivity or rest. The time implied in IB is the time taken for the activity or behavior, and could range from a moment to minutes to hours to years, depending on the duration of the activity, and its associated contexts. For a larger time period, each sub-activity within the behavior will have its own context.

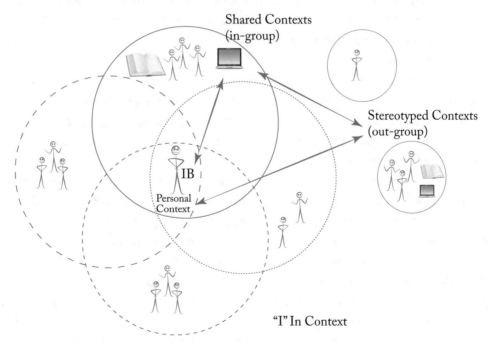

Figure 3.3: Contextual Identity Framework (a)—Personal View of Context (adapted from Agarwal, 2009b and Agarwal, Xu, and Poo, 2009).

This person has multiple social identities as a member of different shared groupings based on age, gender, ethnicity, religion, education, country, socio-economic background, discipline of study/ work, work team, etc. The person might feel more strongly about certain aspects of his/her/their identity (resulting from shared groupings) as compared to the other aspects. For example, one's field of study might be more important to the person than the person's ethnicity. This is indicated by different dotted circles in the figure. The person sees oneself as having a unique identity that draws from these different identities. This personal context of the actor is at the cognitive level (what the actor thinks of themselves), but it could also include aspects such as skills, abilities, personality, etc. that affect one's identity, even if the actor is not consciously aware of it. Also, this sense of one's identity might change with time, and across different situations. For example, when an individual migrates to a different country, the relative degree of attachment or identification with the parent country and with the adopted country might (or might not, in some cases) change after a few years.

For a particular shared grouping such as a team, organization or gender, the person feels a certain sense of kinship toward people within the shared context (the "in-group" people). With members of this shared circle, the actor's interaction is more toward the interpersonal end of the interpersonal-intergroup continuum (Tajfel and Turner, 1979; Figure 3.2). The context can also be shared with artifacts and sources such as books, familiar spaces, computers, phones, etc. Like personal context, the shared context is mostly at the cognitive level (the actor's view of the groups the actor is a part of), but could also include affective/emotional and other subconscious aspects that help the actor feel a sense of kinship with another person or a group, even if the actor cannot always explain the reason for it.

Persons, groups, and even artifacts outside these shared circles/identities of the actor tend to be stereotyped, to varying degrees, and seen from the lens of the groups they belong to, rather than as individuals (toward the intergroup end of the interpersonal-intergroup continuum). The stereotyped context is also likely to be at the cognitive level (the actor's view of people and artifacts that the actor does not identity with).

It is to be noted that all the three levels of context—the personal context, the shared contexts, and the stereotyped contexts—are all as seen and understood by the individual actor. Since they collectively form the actor's context as seen by the actor, they are part of the actor's personal view of the context. This is close to the phenomenological view of context described by Dourish (2004), and "context as constructed meaning—person as context" described by Courtright (2007). Thus, we are talking about the personal context of the actor and the shared context of the actor based on the groups the actor belongs to (as seen by the actor). The shared context is all about the person (based on the groups the actor belongs to), and not any inherent group identity. Similarly, we are talking about the stereotyping the actor engages in upon encountering people outside their shared context. It is based on the actor's perception of that context, and not inherent to the people or the context that are stereotyped.

b.   The Shared View of Context

The shared view of context is similar to the shared grouping/shared context discussed in the previous section, except that, here, the context is as seen by a team or group, as opposed to as seen by the individual actor.

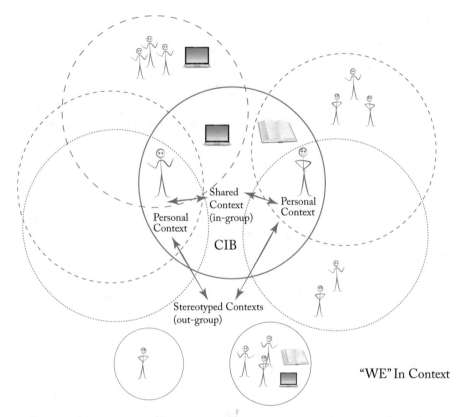

Figure 3.4: Contextual Identity Framework (b)—shared view of context.

Figure 3.4 shows the shared (other terms could be collective, collaborative or social) view of the Contextual Identity Framework. At the center are two or more actors that are part of the shared context, e.g., members of a team, two people from the same hometown, a group of people who speak the same language, etc. Each of these actors has their own individual identity and personal context. They also have one (or more) shared identity which brings them together. They will feel a sense of kinship with each other, and with other members of the group based on that shared identity (though there might be individual differences). This kinship might also be with shared artifacts, e.g., a town library that two people regularly go to, a shared preference for Mac or Windows, or a shared screen space during collaboration. The actors in the shared context will tend to stereotype people, sources, and artifacts outside of their individual personal and their common shared contexts (out-group). The individual personal contexts, the common shared context, and the stereotyped contexts are all as seen by the two or more actors. I therefore refer to it as the "shared view of context." This is closer to the phenomenological view of context described by Dourish (2004), and "socially constructed context: the social actor" described by Courtright (2007). In Figure 3.4, the IB of Figure 3.3 is replaced with CIB—collaborative information behavior. When engaging with information as part of a team, the actors in the team collaborate and cooperate in looking for information, e.g., by sharing a screen or co-browsing, through each may take turns and engage in individual information behaviors (IB) as well. Shah (2012, 2017) provides a detailed treatment of collaborative information seeking and social information seeking respectively. In phenomenological and enthographic approaches to research, and in participant and action research, the researcher would strive to be part of the shared context of the participant, and view the world as the actor(s) views it.

c.   The Stereotyped View of Context

Figure 3.5 shows context as seen by a third person such as a system developer or a positivist researcher, who would prefer objective, quantitative approaches to research. See the discussion on the differences between positivist vs. phenomenological/interpretivist approaches in the beginning paragraphs of Section 1.2.1. When a positivist researcher or system developer tries to study the actor, context is often seen as that which surrounds the actor, or "context as container." This view is almost always stereotyped, and is far from reality. However, it is convenient (the way classification and stereotyping is convenient), and helps the researchers conduct studies on people who they don't necessarily know or understand by virtue of their membership in groups, e.g., doctors, lawyers, students, etc., even though the behavior of an individual doctor might differ from that of another doctor, and even of the same doctor at different points in time. For example, Jansen et al. (2017) analyzed audience interaction with 4,320 online videos in a YouTube channel to see if there are clear audience segments for specific content. Dourish (2004) has criticized this view as the positivist view of context, as have Dervin (1997) and others. Courtright (2007) terms it "context as container." I would argue that even if a researcher were to adopt a phenomenological view (as Dourish suggests), and to adopt ethnographic means of studying the actor in their own context, there would still be a degree of bias, stereotyping, or assuming (we can never fully put oneself in another person's shoes). However, the effect is much more pronounced in positivist research. The stereotyped view of context mostly applies to positivist research, and in system development where the actor is viewed as the user. The three outer circles in Figure 3.5 represent the different methods of studying people or groups by researchers, depending on how much of the actor's personal view of context they consider in their way of gathering data—with phenomenological or ethnographic on the left-hand side, and the more positivist view (where context is simply "all that surrounds") in the two circles on the right. The outer circle is dotted on the left for phenomenological approaches to recognize their explicit orientation toward understanding an interaction from the perspective of the participants in the process, i.e., from the perspective/view of the individual actor or the members of the team. Here, stereotyping is only incidental and not part of the design. In positivist approaches (the two circles on the right), the outer circles are solid, as having a barrier between the researcher and the participant is part of the approach and study design here (with an aim to minimizing bias).

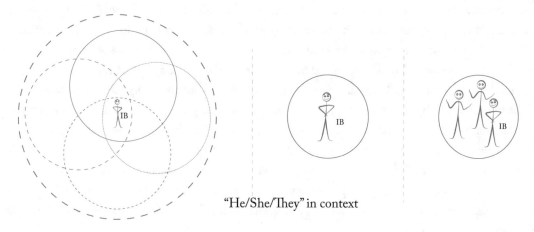

"He/She/They" in context

Figure 3.5: Contextual Identity Framework (c)—stereotyped view of context.

d.   Understanding the Three Views

Thus, the Contextual Identity Framework with its three views—that is, as seen from the eyes of an individual, of a team, and of an outside person (Figures 3.3, 3.4, and 3.5, respectively)—together provide the total picture of context—the elephant in the room. While the individual figures represent a facet each (e.g., the legs, truck, tail, etc. of the elephant), together they constitute the whole elephant.

Tables 3.1 and 3.2 summarize the three views of the Contextual Identity Framework—the personal, the shared, and the stereotyped views. Table 3.1 shows the context levels in each of the three views. In both the personal and shared contexts, there are three levels represented—the individual level of the actor, the in-group (or interpersonal) level, and the in-group/out-group (or intergroup) level. In the personal view of context (Figure 3.3), the personal context is at the individual level, the many shared contexts of the actor (based on age, race, nationality, gender, profession, degree of familiarity, etc.) are at the in-group level, and the stereotyped contexts of people and artifacts are at the in-group/out-group level, creating a feeling of separateness or differentiation. The shared view (Figure 3.4) consists of the personal contexts of the actors in the team at the individual level. At the in-group level are the many shared contexts of the actors in the team with other people/artifacts and the shared contexts with each other. At the in-group/out-group level reside the stereotyped contexts (as seen by the actors in the team or a shared group) of people and artifacts/ information sources (e.g., books, repositories, websites, databases, etc.) that the members of the team don't feel a kinship with and tend to judge as "outsiders". In the stereotyped view of context (Figure 3.5), i.e., context as seen from the eyes of a third person like a positivist researcher or a system developer, everything is stereotyped. To some level, it would also apply to interpretivist researchers because no matter how hard one tries to put oneself in the other's shoes, there will always be a degree of separateness between the experiences of the actor in a situation and the experiences of those studying or looking at the situation from afar. A similar feeling of exasperation was voiced by a Facebook friend: "While I appreciate the concept behind someone telling me they understand, the truth is that no one understands what you go through or who you really are and no one has the right to belittle you by saying that they know your pain or struggle—no one does—let's keep things honest and just say 'I care' rather than 'I know'…" (personal Facebook feed—Anima Nair, July 29, 2017). The quote argues that we can never fully "know" another person. At the individual level, the researcher may be studying the stereotyped (personal) contexts of an actor or a sample of actors.

However, noted sociological phenomenologist Alfred Schütz has an interesting take on this, as he explains the problem of intersubjective understanding. His translator George Walsh writes in the introduction to Schütz's work:

> "…the genuine understanding of the other person is a more concrete thing. It is a type of perception. This does not mean that we can directly intuit another person's subjective experiences. What it does mean is that we can intentionally grasp those experiences because we assume that [the person's] facial expressions and…gestures are a "field of expression" for [the person's] inner life. This is what Schütz calls the "bodily presence" or "corporeal givenness" of the partner. The crucial factor here is simultaneity. We sense that the other person's stream of consciousness is flowing along a track that is temporally parallel with our own. The two duration-flows are synchronized, and, in social interaction, they can become interlocked. This is the essence of the interpersonal relationship, and it is basic to our knowledge of other people. Of course, we are at a certain disadvantage in our knowledge of other people's inner life. In a certain sense this knowledge is indirect and discontinuous. But Schütz makes the interesting observation that there is another sense in which we can know other people better than we can know ourselves. For we can "watch" other people's subjective experiences as they actually occur, whereas we have to wait for our own to elapse in order to peer at them as they recede into the past" (Walsh, 1967, pp. xxv–xxvi; Schütz, 1967).

In our current world increasingly filled with interactions using text, emoticons, and images in messages or social media, face-to-face interactions leading to simultaneity are increasingly rare and far-between, and the "bodily presence" or "corporeal givenness" not always there, with notifications from messages and phone calls or emails being a constant feature of our day-to-day lives. Thus, the likelihood of another person's context being stereotyped remains high. However, interpretivist researchers and ethnographic approaches can strive to achieve this level of "corporal givenness" described by Schütz.

Table 3.1: Context levels in each of the three views of context in Contextual Identity Framework

	Personal View of Context	Shared View of Context	Stereotyped View of Context
Usefulness of	Useful for the interpretive researcher (or system designer) when understanding human-information interaction from the perspective of the individual actor in the process	Useful for the interpretive researcher (or system designer) when understanding human-information interaction from the perspective of the team members in the process	Used by the positivist researcher (or system developer) when studying human-information interaction involving the actor or a team, by keeping the researcher out of view
Individual level	Personal context • *My view of myself and my contexts*	Personal contexts • *Our individual differences*	Stereotyped (personal) contexts • *Outside person's view of my context*
In-group level (inter-personal)	Shared contexts • *My view of us and our contexts*	Shared contexts • *Our commonalities*	Stereotyped (shared) contexts • *Outside person's view of our context*
In-group/out-group level (intergroup)	Stereotyped contexts • *My view of he/she/ they/it and their contexts*	Stereotyped contexts • *Our view of he/she/ they/it and their contexts*	Stereotyped contexts • *Outside person's view of his/her/their context*

Table 3.2 summarizes the three views of context in the Contextual Identity Framework. I adapt parts of the table from Agarwal, Xu, and Poo (2009). The table provides the description of each view, the people it applies to, and the minds it resides in (whether of the actor or an external positivist researcher or system developer). It also identifies the degree of assumed objectivity in each view (ranging from the subjective to the objective), and whether each view is reality vs. simplification. It identifies the theoretical approaches and research methods for studying each view. The researcher may choose to interview, observe, or ethnographically study members of a team to see patterns of their shared contexts; or the researcher may study the stereotyped contexts of the people and artifacts outside the immediate in-group levels of the actor or team being studied. For personal

and shared views of context, the theoretical approach will be phenomenological (Dourish, 2004), with generally qualitative research methods used to study the actor(s) involved. For the stereotyped view of context, quantitative methods such as surveys, experiments, data analytics, etc. will likely be used. The researcher may also straddle between the personal/shared views on one end and the stereotyped view on the other end by using mixed methods, or qualitative methods such as interviews, case study, etc. (especially if the sample size is small, and *how* and *why* questions are to be answered). When a method such as ethnography is carried out over an extended period of time, the researcher can get an insider's view of the actors and phenomenon under study, but in such a case, the researcher ceases to be an outsider and becomes part (to varying degrees) of the group under study. Thus, the shared view of context (Figure 3.4) then becomes applicable.

Table 3.2: Summary of three views of context in Contextual Identity Framework			
Context Views	**Personal View of Context**	**Shared View of Context**	**Stereotyped View of Context**
Person Viewing	**I**	**We**	**Outside Person**
Description	My view of my context (personal, shared, and stereotyped); everything with respect to my activity is my context	Our view of our personal, shared and stereotyped contexts	His/her/their view of my (or someone else's) context
Who does it apply to?	Context of a person A seen from the eyes of person A	Context of a group (or groups) consisting of A, B, and C seen from the eyes of persons A, B, and C	Context of a person A (or of a group A, B, and C) seen from the eyes of person Z
Where does it reside?	My mind (personal, internal)	Our minds (runs through a group due to the shared identity of the group)	Outside mind (external; his/his/their perception of my, our or someone else's mind(s))

Degree of assumed objectivity	Subjective (cognitive, affective, psychological dimensions of person A)	Subjective (cognitive, affective, psychological dimensions of persons A, B, and C with a shared common ground)	Usually seen as objective (that which surrounds the "cognitive, affective and psychological dimensions" of a person A, or of a group A, B, and C)
Reality vs. simplification	Reality/complex	Reality/complex (trying to find commonality/ sense of security in common norms, values or *worldview*—Chatman, 2000)	A convenient simplification which is not reflective of actual reality (a research and everyday life imperative; important for design of search systems)
Usage for	Useful for the interpretive researcher (or system designer) when understanding human-information interaction from the perspective of the individual actor in the process	Useful for the interpretive researcher (or system designer) when understanding human-information interaction from the perspective of the team members in the process	Used by the positivist researcher (or system developer) when studying human-information interaction involving the actor or a team, by keeping the researcher out of view
Theoretical approach to studying context view	Phenomenological	Phenomenological	Positivist
Suitable research methodology	Generally qualitative	Generally qualitative	Generally quantitative
Suitable research methods	E.g., journals, self-reflection, action research	E.g., individual and group interviews, ethnography, focus groups, reflections, action research	E.g., surveys, experiments, data analytics, etc.

In Figure 3.6, I represent the Contextual Identity Framework using three pyramids (representing the three views of context), where each pyramid has three faces (representing the three levels discussed above in Table 3.2). In the personal view of context, the personal context is the strongest (I would know the most about myself). Thus, this face is represented by bold lines. In the shared view of context, the relationship shared by two or more individuals in a collaboration, team or group is the most important. Thus, here, the shared contexts are marked as bold. In all the three views, the stereotyped contexts are the weakest (since we have the least knowledge of them). These are, thus, represented by dotted lines.

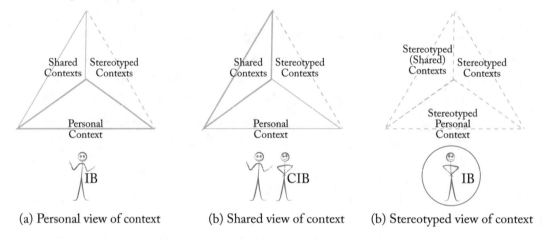

(a) Personal view of context   (b) Shared view of context   (b) Stereotyped view of context

Figure 3.6: Contextual Identity Framework (three pyramids).

In Figure 3.7, the Contextual Identity Framework is represented in a single nine-faced nonagon, or an umbrella shape. This figure helps see the three views of context, and the three levels of each view in a single shape. This is akin to seeing the entire elephant at one go. A set of three contiguous triangles or faces represents a particular view of context. Here, the bold and dotted lines have the same representation as in Figure 3.6. In both Figure 3.6 and Figure 3.7, the personal view is the view of the actor engaged in information behavior (represented by the stick figure with IB). The shared view is the view of two (or more) actors engaged in collaborative (and including individual) information behavior. The stereotyped view is the view of the positivist researcher or an outside person. This is represented by surrounding the actor with a container or circle. This person views the actor from outside this circle.

Let us further understand the views with the help of an example. Say you are engaged in some information behavior, e.g., seeking information related to a project you are working on. I'll call you "you" (you may substitute this with your name). You also have a close friend who is helping you with the project. Let us call this person "friend" (you may replace this with your friend's name). You also have other friends and family, and people you like or follow. Let us call them "close ones" (think of one or two people among your close friends, family, or colleagues). There are some people you don't like or do not know much about. Let us call them "others." Think of one or two persons who you don't know much about or do not like for some reason.

The personal view of context will be your view of your own context. It will consist of you, and your situation, the project you are engaged in and the information you need to find (your personal context). This view will also include you and your friend, and you and your close ones (all those who are a part of your shared contexts). There will also be the others who you don't know much about (your stereotyped contexts).

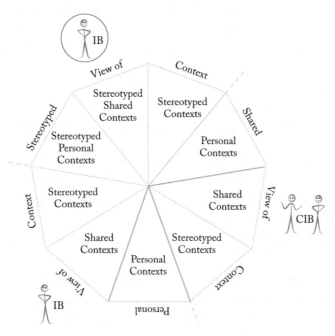

Figure 3.7: Contextual Identity Framework (umbrella).

The shared view of context will be the combined view of the common context between you and your friend when you are engaged in information seeking for the project that you both are working on. This view will consist of your individual differences and particular likes and dislikes (your personal contexts), your commonalities based on your interest in the project, and other things that you share in common, e.g., gender, food habits, etc. (your shared contexts), things that you both share with other people (e.g., the shared contexts between you and your close ones), as well as your individual and combined views of the others that you do not like or do not know much about. Here, the shared and stereotyped contexts could also consist of inanimate objects such as books, movies, websites, etc.

The stereotyped view of context is what your teacher or supervisor (we will call this person the boss) at work thinks of either you individually, or of you and your friend as a team. This will include what the boss knows and thinks about you (the stereotyped personal context), what the boss thinks about your team with your friend (the stereotyped shared context), and what the boss thinks or knows about the other people that you do not like or do not know much about (the stereotyped contexts).

The importance of recognizing different views (whether the actor's or another person's) is also alluded to by Sonnenwald (1999) when she says that difficulties arise when attempting to exhaustively characterize a context from a single point of view, and instead recommends digging deeper. She cites the example provided by Simon (1981), who pointed out that "a bird's eye view of an ant walking between two points along a sandy beach shows a seemingly erratic path. It is only when we view the ant's path from a three-dimensional perspective and notice the hills and valleys caused by the grains of sand that we begin to realize that the ant's path is ingenious, not erratic" (Sonnenwald, 1999, p. 179).

3.3   DELINEATING THE ELEMENTS OF CONTEXT

Now that we have sought to delineate the boundaries of context, using the personal and shared views of the actor, and the external view of that of the positivist researcher or system developer, let us define the views further by identifying the elements and variables that make up context. Identifying the elements that constitute context will then help us to better investigate context in information behavior. We can then place these elements and variables within the three views of the Contextual Identity Framework.

Context is multi-dimensional (Dervin, 1997) and comprises many elements. Ingwersen and Järvelin (2005) emphasize that contexts "may be of social, cultural or organizational nature, associated with objects, systems and domains, searchers' work and daily life tasks and emotional interests, intentionality and preferences" (p. 306). Ingwersen (2005) says that context includes "time, place, history of interaction, task in hand, and a range of other factors that are not given explicitly but are implicit in the interaction and ambient environment" (p. 6). He lists several elements of context that are potentially significant to information retrieval, a type of information behavior. These include work or daily life task or interest features, searcher features, interaction features, system features, document features, environmental/physical features, and temporal features. Sonnenwald (1999) also cites examples of elements and variables (which she terms attributes) that researchers have used to describe contexts, including place, time, goals, tasks, systems, situations, processes, organizations, and types of participants.

It is important here to distinguish between elements and variables. We can define elements as parts of the whole that make up context, and variables as attributes that help measure each of those parts. For example, if the task at hand is an element of context, variables associated with this element could be the urgency or complexity of the task. Similarly, if an actor or a seeker is an element, the age or experience or degree of knowledge of the actor are the variables associated with that element. Thus, while an element on its own is not measurable, various measurable attributes of the element can be referred to as variables. In this section, we are more concerned about delineating the elements comprising context. We list variables in Section 3.4.

In Section 2.2.3, we identified various variables pertaining to context from a literature review of empirical studies on information seeking and behavior. The major contextual elements identified from the literature that have a relationship with and influence information behavior are: environment, task/activity/problem/situation, need/information required, actor, source/system/channel, actor-source relationship, and time/space. These elements are listed in Figure 3.8. The figure shows that all these elements can be seen from the view of the actor (personal view of context), a team or group (the shared view of context) or an outside person (stereotyped view of context). The treatment given to each element in the different views will, however, be different. For example, in the personal view, the actor element is linked with the personal identity of the actor. Thus, it is bound to be more intimate. In the shared view, there would be more than one actor, with individual identities, as well as shared identity and common ground. For conducting interpretive research, the researcher will aim to identify with the personal or shared views of context. In the stereotyped view, the actor would be an individual or group being studied or stereotyped, e.g., one or more research participants in an experiment or survey, or target audiences in a search engine or app design.

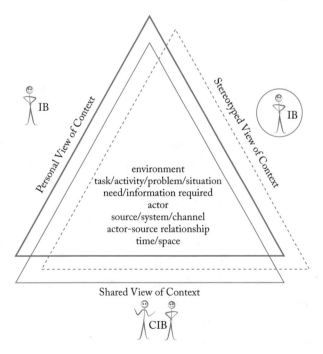

Figure 3.8: Elements of context.

Let us now try to place each of these context elements within the three levels (personal context, shared contexts and stereotyped contexts) in one of the three views of context. This is a loose categorization as an exercise to see where these contextual elements would best fit within the contextual levels. This would help provide a bird's eye view of the major elements that potentially make up the context of an actor's information behavior. As an example, we will look at the personal view of context (see Figure 3.9). Similar figures can be drawn for the other two views of context as well.

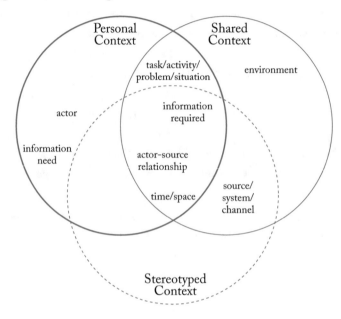

Figure 3.9: Placing context elements within levels in personal view of context.

Each of the three overlapping circles in Figure 3.9 represents a particular level of context in one of the three views of the Contextual Identity Framework (we use the personal view of context as an example in the figure). The cognitive actor is placed within the personal context, as all context is personal when seen from the eyes of the actor. However, depending on culture (collectivistic vs. individualistic; see Hofstede, 1980) and the degree to which an individual identifies with a community or with others, the actor could be part of the shared contexts as well (in which case, the "actor" label in the figure would move in the common area intersecting the personal and shared context circles). A mystical person may see his/her group identity as all of humanity, or a blurring of distinction between the personal and the shared contexts. Another actor may be very clear about what is personal vs. what is shared. (In the shared view of context, where context is seen by a team or group of people, the actor is also part of the shared context of the team.)

While the actor is situated in one's personal context, the actor is influenced by and identifies with shared contexts and elements that are part of it. This would include the surrounding environment, whether at home, work or outside. When faced with an information need, the actor interacts with an information source to try and get the desired information.

This source could be a person (friend/colleague), with whom the actor interacts either face-to-face, through synchronous communication such as phone or chat, or over email or other asynchronous messaging. The source could also be online or electronic, such as a website, database, repository, or other system. It could also be a physically printed book or manual. See Agarwal (2011) and Agarwal, Xu, and Poo (2011) for further discussion on source and channel types. The information seeking behavior exhibited in this process depends upon the degree of closeness between the actor and the source, i.e., whether the actor views this source at the level of one's: (1) personal context (e.g., looking from memory, personal collection, etc.; see Krikelas, 1983); (2) shared contexts (great degree of closeness, kinship or familiarity with the source—which could be a person, book, or electronic source); or (3) stereotyped contexts (elements that are outside the actor's comfort zone or shared context).

The shared contexts of the actor might consist of his/her work or team environment, his/her friends and family, or other domains of human activity or everyday life that the actor is surrounded by, or surrounds oneself by. The degree to which these are part of the shared contexts depends on the degree to which the actor identifies with them, is familiar and comfortable with them, and sees them as a part of oneself. Examples could be a close friend or a colleague or a book one really likes. Those members of the organization that the actor doesn't know or identify with are part of the stereotyped contexts. Here, examples could be getting some information from a professor a student doesn't know well, a reference librarian, or a colleague that one does not particularly like. The sources of information could be interpersonal, online sources, or a book from the library, and could be accessed/reached through channels such as face-to-face, email, phone/chat, etc. Krikelas (1983) classifies information sources as internal (e.g., the actor's memory or direct observations) and external to the searcher. The external sources would be the ones placed at the level of the shared or stereotyped contexts, depending on the relationship of the actor with the source. These would include direct interpersonal contact or recorded literature. Krikelas' "internal" sources that reside within the actor's mind would lie at the level of personal context in Figure 3.9.

The actor-source relationship is a continuum; the actor might place a particular source in between the two circles of stereotyped and shared contexts. To highlight this interaction, in Figure 3.9, this context element is placed in the intersection between all three levels of context. The source/system/channel element is placed in the intersection of the shared and stereotyped contexts, and could move either way within these. This is different from the placement of the environment which surrounds the actor (the actor is situated in the environment), and is thus part of the actor's shared context.

Thus, I have based the placement of a particular element at a particular level of context on the most likely placement at a particular point in time. In doing so, I have also drawn from Tajfel and Turner's (1979) social identity theory. I have placed other elements in the intersections of the circles as they result from the interaction of elements which might be part of different circles. For example, the task/activity/problem/situation falls under the interaction of personal and shared contexts because a task or problem situation (that requires information seeking or another form of information behavior) often arises when an environment of which we are a part faces a problem, which may trickle down to us in one form or another (based on which, we start interacting with information). Even when we are looking for information to satisfy our curiosity (an artifact of personal context), our curiosity is often aroused by an external stimulant in the environment where we operate. The resulting information need is placed in the personal context circle, as need occurs inside the person's head (even though the shared context contributed to the need to complete the larger task or activity at hand).

The actual information required results from an interaction of the three levels of context (the environment giving rise to the task, the actor and one's information need, and the source that has the information). Thus, I place it at the intersection of the three levels. The other contributing elements are the time and space for interaction, which I also place at the intersection of the three levels.

In Figure 3.9 and in the previous discussion, we have concentrated on the personal view of context, which is the context of the actor as seen from the eyes of the actor. In the shared view of context (the context of a team as seen from the eyes of the members of the team), the actor elements would reside both at the level of the individual personal contexts, as well as at the level of the shared context between them. The information need would be at the level of the shared context (the shared need of the team), though there would also be the need of the individual actors even when doing a collaborative task (which would be at the level of the personal contexts).

The placement of elements within the stereotyped view of context is not likely to change from that in the personal view of context. However, what changes is how these elements (and specific variables within these elements, which we discuss in the next section) are treated. This is because there is a difference between what is experienced by the actor (and studied by the inter-pretive researcher) vs. what is studied by the positivist researcher. In the personal and shared view of contexts, the contextual elements are experienced by the actor or the team respectively. However, in the stereotyped view of context, the different contextual elements pertaining to the actor, the actor's information need, task, environment, etc. are studied by an outside positivist researcher. The positivist researcher might focus on actor attributes or variables such as age, sex, profession or other demographics, while the actor might be more concerned with one's thoughts, feelings, and coping mechanisms when engaged in a task. Table 3.3 summarizes the placement of contextual elements within each of the three levels of the three views of the Contextual Identity Framework.

Table 3.3: Placing context elements within levels in each of the three views of context

Context Views	Personal View of Context			Shared View of Context			Stereotyped View of Context		
Context Levels	pl cxt	sh cxts	st cxts	pl cxts	sh cxts	st cxts	st (pl) cxt	st (sh) cxts	st cxts
environment		*			*			*	
task / activity / problem / situation	*	*		*	*		*	*	
information need	*			*	*		*		
information required	*	*	*	*	*	*	*	*	*
actor	*			*	*		*		
source / system / channel		*	*		*	*		*	*
actor-source relationship	*	*	*	*	*	*	*	*	*
time / space	*	*	*	*	*	*	*	*	*
pl = personal | sh = shared | st = stereotyped | cxt = context | cxts = contexts									

When studying the information seeking behavior of an actor, the different contextual elements interact with each other. In Figure 3.10 (adapted from Agarwal, 2011), we look at one possible scenario of the interaction among context elements when the actor is looking for information. This workflow of interaction would be different for other types of information behavior such as serendipitous information encountering, information avoidance, etc. Since the study in this example is from the point of view of a (positivist) researcher (as opposed to that of the actor or a group), we will use the stereotyped view of context. In this view, the personal and shared context levels are stereotyped (i.e., seen from the view of an external researcher). See Figure 3.10. In the figure, the numbers 1, 2, and 3 are used to indicate the sequence of flow.

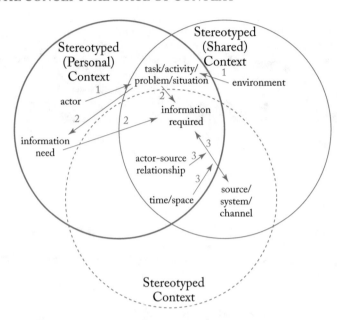

Figure 3.10: Interaction among context elements in stereotyped view of context of information seeking behavior.

From the point of the view of the positivist researcher, the environment of a seeker's shared context plays upon the actor to bring about a task/activity/problem/situation requiring a need for information (indicated by the arrows with 1 in the figure). This gives rise to knowledge or information that needs to be sought from a source (indicated by the arrows with 2). The actor then approaches a source (personal or impersonal) for this information. Depending upon the time and place of interaction between the actor and the source, and the relationship shared by the actor and the source, the source passes the knowledge sought to the seeker (indicated by the arrows with 3 in Figure 3.10). This is an example of a simple workflow of interaction between context elements. There might be multiple cycles or processes in different workflows that might involve a different sequence of context elements. Also, the workflow would change depending on the specific type of information behavior engaged in by an actor.

3.4   DELINEATING THE VARIABLES COMPRISING CONTEXT

As we discussed at the beginning of the previous section, elements are parts of a whole, while variables are specific attributes of those elements which are measurable in research studies. We will now list specific variables pertaining to the different contextual elements that we identified from the literature review of empirical studies in Chapter 2. We will then attempt to place these variables under the respective contextual elements within each context element of a particular view of context. When studying individual actor(s), the interpretive researcher could place these variables in the personal view of context. When studying groups or collectives, the interpretive researcher could place these in the shared view of context. Since positivist studies utilize the perspective of an outside researcher, the positive researcher would find it useful to place these variables in the stereotyped view of context when studying individuals or groups.

Table 3.4 lists the variables for the different context elements identified. The sources for these variables can be seen from the various tables in Section 2.2.3. This list of variables, while long, is not necessarily exhaustive. Different terms can be used to denote or label the phenomenon measured by a particular variable. Also, there could be other variables not in the table that could relate to a particular context element. In the table, I have *italicized* examples of those variables (particularly from the actor and source/system/channel contextual elements) that are likely to remain relatively stable across situations.

Table 3.4: Context elements and variables	
Context Elements	**Context Variables**
Environment	• Type (organization, social network, culture, physical environment) • Organizational structure; diversity, flexibility, goals; organizational decision-making style; resources, support • Influences of stakeholders and work colleagues; collective discourse of community; employees' familiarity with each other; *shared context* • *Information culture; organizational climate; cultural differences in information environments and practices; culture* • Embodiment
Task/activity/ problem/ situation	• Type, nature, goal, dimension, characteristic • Specificity • Domain or topic • Stage, step, phase • Complexity, difficulty, uncertainty, non-routineness, intellectual demand • Importance, urgency • Interdependency • Engagement
Need	• Trigger (job and task type, everyday life) • Changing nature

Information Required	• Judgments of "enough" • Importance and utility • Tacitness • Observability • Systemic nature
Actor	• Demographics (academic background, age, gender) • Coping style; cognitive ability/style; perceptual speed; visualization abilities; personality—"it's mine!", extroversion; identity; problem-solving style; metacognitive monitoring; risk aversion; reciprocation wariness • Habits; reading habits; hobbies • Disability • Work domain; work role; tenure in position; tenure in organization; social role • Experience, domain knowledge, knowledge state, impact of previous information seen, understanding; pre-search confidence; information literacy; cognitive state • Search skills; prior experience with system; technical aptitude • Mood; information overload; attitude toward task; affective state • Interest; motivation; curiosity; academic orientation; learning orientation; need for achievement
Source/system/channel	• Type (interpersonal, impersonal), dimension • Quality; authority; appropriateness; uniqueness; people—skills, job roles; reliability; usefulness; documents—author, style; currency; system—interface, customizability, functionality, features, interactivity, search interaction method, information objects; device—aesthetics; apps—variety • Accessibility, speed, place, format, physical proximity, impersonal—ease of use; cost; communication difficulty; understandability; device—portability, embodiment
Actor-source relationship	• Social risk, embarrassment, loss of face, revelation of incompetence • Degree of comfort, quality • Expectation • Degree of familiarity with source/system
Time/space	• Time of interaction, immediacy, time constraints, time pressure, estimation of time needed, duration, time of day/week/year, before-during-after, actions in relation to time, synchronicism (synchronous, asynchronous) • Place of interaction, spatial location, functional place and space, artefacts • History of past interaction

In Figure 3.11, the frameworks of Figure 3.9, Figure 3.10, and Table 3.4 are used as a basis to arrive at a framework of context elements with variables. I have used the stereotyped view of context as an example in the figure. It would be applicable to positivist researchers. To accommodate the variables names for all elements in the figure, I only included the major categories for variables in the figure. Details and alternatives for those variable categories are in Table 3.4. The figure could be replicated for personal and shared views of context, which would be more applicable to interpretive researchers. The researcher needs to carefully consider the actor in the process being studied. The actor may be an individual or may be a group. If it is a group, then both the personal views and shared view of context of the actors engaged in information behavior would be useful in the study design.

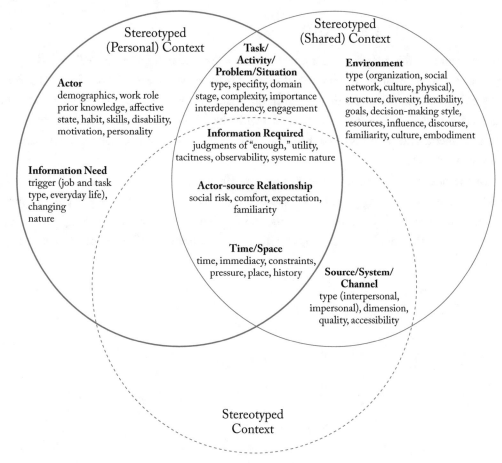

Figure 3.11: Context elements with variables (in stereotyped view of context).

Figure 3.11 is useful in understanding what is a part of the actor and what attributes are detached from the actor (as seen from the point of view of the positivist researcher). The divisions could also be from the person's or team's point of view (as used by the interpretivist researcher). While not exhaustive, these variables (in Figure 3.11 and Table 3.4) serve as examples of context in common usage in past empirical studies of human information behavior. Researchers designing studies in information behavior will be able to get a quick overview of various context variables and their placement within the context levels of any particular view of the Contextual Identity Framework. The variables can serve as useful moderators, but could also be incorporated as independent, mediating or dependent variables in the design of quantitative studies. They would also help in identifying areas of focus for interpretive studies. Both the Contextual Identity Framework and the frameworks of elements and variables should together help provide a basis for further research in the meaning, role and boundaries of context in human information behavior.

3.5   CHAPTER SUMMARY

At the beginning of this chapter, we set out to answer a few research questions: What does context really mean? How do we map the conceptual space of context? What are the boundaries of context? What are the variables that make up context in information behavior and that can be incorporated into research studies? We looked at boundaries with the help of views and levels of context. We looked at elements and variables of context, and positioned them within specific levels in particular views of context.

In the next chapter, we will discuss how we can use the frameworks arrived at to design research studies incorporating context, the importance of the notion of stereotyped context, movement between shared and stereotyped contexts, and the dynamism of context through overlapping and continuous reshaping. In Chapter 5, we will arrive at a unified definition of context in information behavior.

CHAPTER   4

Discussion

In the first two chapters, we looked at various conceptualizations on context by different researchers—both theoretical and empirical. I put forth my own thinking in the preceding chapter. We arrived at a number of frameworks to delineate the boundaries, and to identify the elements and variables of context in information behavior. Let us now briefly discuss how these can help in the design of empirical research studies. We will then look at stereotyped context and the movement between stereotyped and shared contexts. Here, I bring in the discussion from social phenomenology and the seminal work of Alfred Schütz in social science. Finally, we will also look at context overlap and the continuous reshaping of context.

4.1   DESIGNING RESEARCH STUDIES INCORPORATING CONTEXT

Empirical research in information behavior can involve collection of data using one or more quantitative methods such as a survey, experiment or other qualitative, or mixed methods. The framework of context elements with variables (Figure 3.11 and Table 3.4) provides a list of variables that apply to different elements and views of context relating to an actor's information behavior. While not all variables would apply to a single study, a researcher conducting a quantitative study could easily pick a set of variables from the framework and design a research model for an empirical study incorporating context. In any study, most of the contextual elements of interest are likely to remain the same, as a study is likely to involve an actor, the actor's environment, the task at hand, etc. Thus, variables for a study would typically involve the personal context, the shared context, and the stereotyped context once the independent, dependent, mediating/moderating and control variables are considered. For a discussion on specific types of variables, refer to the *Encyclopedia of Research Design* (Salkind, 2010). Trochim (2006) explains independent and dependent variables. MacKinnon (2011) provides a detailed treatment on mediating and moderating variables. In interpretive studies, the elements and variables can help in the formation of research questions, interview questions, or point the researcher toward areas to focus when gathering data.

For example, in a quantitative study, we could pick a set of variables pertaining to the following elements of context—actor, task, environment, actor-source relationship, and source/channel—to investigate their effect on the use of a source by the actor, and to see what contextual elements affect source use. The focus could be to help answer whether source quality or source accessibility is of greater importance when a person chooses particular information sources (e.g., a friend or colleague to consult face-to-face, a person to reach over email, a person on phone or online chat, a physical book or a manual, or a website or repository; see Agarwal, 2011).

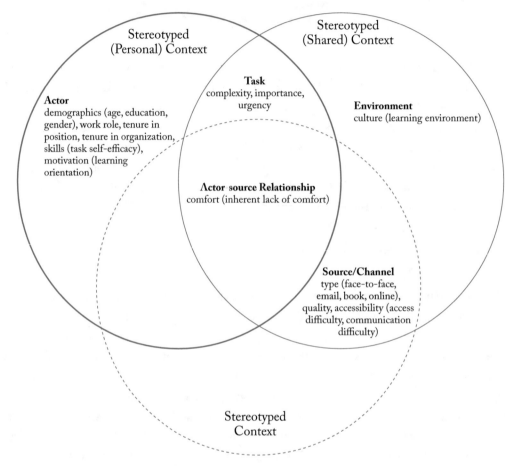

Figure 4.1: Picking variables from the framework and table to apply to an empirical study.

I used one of the initial drafts of the framework of context variables (Agarwal, 2009a) to design such a study, which was published as Agarwal, Xu, and Poo (2011). The published empirical model (which would map to the variables of Figure 4.1) is reproduced below. A few of the variables in Figure 4.1 were control variables which we included in the study but did not incorporate in the causal research model of Figure 4.2.

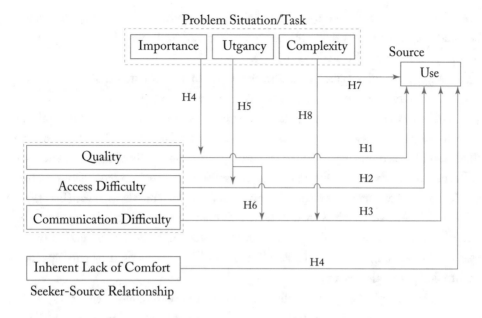

Figure 4.2: Empirical research model (Agarwal, Xu, and Poo, 2011).

We measured the actor variables (part of the personal context) relating to demographics, work role, task self-efficacy and learning orientation in the survey of 352 working people that we carried out, but we did not include these in the hypotheses. We also included the environmental variable (part of the shared context) of whether their workplace had a favorable learning environment or not as a control variable. We designed the study to see the effect of the relative costs and benefits of particular types of sources on the use of those sources, to fulfill a current task or project at work. We measured the benefit using the source quality variable and the cost using the access difficulty and communication difficulty variables. We included all these as independent variables in the study. Depending on the kinship or familiarity that the actor feels for particular sources or types of sources, they could lie within the circles of shared contexts or stereotyped contexts of Figure 4.1. The relationship between the actor or seeker and the source is also important to the use of a source. We included this as an independent variable, to see its effect on the dependent variable of source use. The direct effects that we hypothesized are indicated by the arrows H1–H4 in Figure 4.2. The variables relating to the problem situation or task at hand (resulting from the interaction of the personal and the shared context) were important moderators that we included in the study. These were task importance, task urgency and task complexity. We included these to see if the effect of the cost and benefit calculation by an actor on source use would be moderated by the relative importance of the task (which would require source quality to be important), or by the task's urgency (where source accessibility might become most important) or complexity. Since these are moderators, we have shown the arrows from these variables to affect the relationship between the independent variables and the dependent variable of source use. You can find more details of the study, as well as its findings, in Agarwal, Xu, and Poo (2011).

We can pick up more recent quantitative studies to see how its variables relate to the ones included in the framework of context elements with variables (Figure 3.11 and Table 3.4). For example, Kiseleva et al. (2016) investigate the degree to which users are satisfied with intelligent voice-controlled personal assistants such as Cortana, Google Now, Siri, and Alexa, and the factors that affect user satisfaction. They included 60 participants from a technology company in an experiment. The dependent variable in the study was user satisfaction. Their independent variables related to the task and actor elements from the framework of context elements with variables (Figure 3.11 and Table 3.4). They had variables of task type, task complexity, and task completion. Their actor variables included the demographic information about gender, language and education, as well as the actor's ability to complete a task (task self-efficacy). The sources used by participants were the voice-controlled personal assistants.

In another example, Crescenzi, Kelly, and Azzopardi (2016) conducted a study with 45 participants to investigate how time constraints and system delays impacted the user experience during information search. Their independent variables related to the task, information required, actor, source, and time elements from the framework of context elements with variables (Figure 3.11 and Table 3.4). The task variables related to task specificity/definition, task difficulty and complexity, task urgency/speed, and task importance/accuracy. Their dependent variable measured whether the information required to complete the task was enough. The actor variables included prior domain knowledge and interest in the topic, as well as metacognitive monitoring. The source/system variables included system speed. The time variables included time pressure.

There are examples of qualitative studies as well that show how the variables investigated in these related to the ones included in Figure 3.11 and Table 3.4. In the second half of Section 2.2.2, we discussed multiple qualitative studies that used interviews, ethnographic studies, observation, content analysis, as well as mixed-methods. As an example of a qualitative study, Anderson (2005) used participant observation of two researchers over a two-year period to create a multi-layered narrative by weaving together different ethnographic stories. The purpose was to focus on the actors' research goals rather than on retrieval tasks to more fully understand the relationship between their ultimate research goals and the articulation of those goals in their interactions with information systems. The actor variables she identified were prior knowledge, understanding, and research goals. The actor-source relationship variable was expectations about source. The tasks investigated were research tasks and search tasks.

While we are trying to relate published studies to the framework of context elements with variables (Figure 3.11 and Table 3.4) here, the framework will be useful in helping pick variables from different context element categories in the design of studies investigating some form of information behavior. However, while the variable listing is useful, what is the importance of the circles of stereotyped and shared contexts? Let us discuss this below.

4.2   STEREOTYPED CONTEXT AND THE MOVEMENT BETWEEN STEREOTYPED AND SHARED CONTEXTS

One of the central concepts that has emerged from the Contextual Identity Framework is the notion of stereotyped context, and the movement between stereotyped and shared context. This flows naturally from my theoretical lens of Tajfel and Turner (1979)'s social identity theory. In Figure 3.2 (Section 3.2.3), we saw a continuum. One end of the continuum shows people engaging fully in interpersonal or in-group behavior where their interaction is fully determined by their interpersonal relationships and individual characteristics, and not judged on the basis of the social groups or categories that other individuals belong to. The other extreme of the continuum shows people engaging fully in intergroup or in-group/out-group behavior where their interaction is fully determined by their membership in various social groups or categories and not at all affected by the interpersonal relationships among the people interacting. The reality, of course, is somewhere in between, and often very fluid. A little argument or misunderstanding can draw people apart, and people sometimes begin judging even those that they know well on the basis of their group memberships. On the other hand, a little gesture of forgiveness or an act of love, acceptance or respect can get people to forget the "otherness" of people and accept them easily as one of theirs. An advertisement by the Dutch brewing company Heineken International sought to demonstrate that people with opposing social and political views could also come together and accept their differences, once they have spent some time and gotten to know each other as individuals. Published on YouTube in April 2017, the 4-minute video had already garnered more than 14 million views in less than 4 months (14,142,708 views with 64,880 likes and 4,126 dislikes as of August 13, 2017) (Heineken International, 2017).

In the framework of the elements of context (Figure 3.9) and the framework of context elements with variables (Figure 3.11 and Table 3.4), this continuum of Figure 3.2 is denoted by the actor-source relationship. This relationship determines whether a particular information source (a friend or a colleague, a book, online resource, etc., reached through a particular channel such as face-to-face, email, or voice/video, and/or through a computer, phone, or tablet) is viewed by the actor as being part of the actor's shared context (greater level of closeness or kinship) or as a stereotyped context.

Do note that all three levels of context (personal, shared, and stereotyped) are stereotyped as far as the positivist researcher is concerned, because the researcher is getting an outsider's view. In Figure 3.11 and Figure 4.1, each level of context is denoted by the word "stereotyped" preceding it. However, within the stereotyped view of context, there are the level of shared and stereotyped contexts which are from the point of view of the actor (but being studied by an outside researcher). The interpretivist researcher would focus more on the personal and shared views of context.

While the actor-source relationship may remain fairly fixed in certain instances for certain people (depending on how open the actor is, or how comfortable the situation is to allow the status quo to remain), it may also change quite easily. In Table 3.4, this is represented by several variables: social risk, embarrassment, loss of face, revelation of incompetence, degree of comfort, quality expectation, and degree of familiarity with the source or system. Degree of familiarity, for instance, can easily change once an actor undergoes training with the system, or starts using the system more for a task at hand. In Agarwal, Xu, and Poo (2011), I had used the variable "inherent lack of comfort" (Figure 4.1 and 4.2) as an overarching variable to measure the actor-source relationship. We operationalized it with the survey questions: "I would be nervous to use this source for information in solving this problem; I would be embarrassed to use this source for information; I might be thought as incompetent if I use this source for information; I would not feel comfortable using this source for this problem; Using this source will not be nice for my image—the way another person sees me; and using this source will not be nice for my self-image—the way I see myself" (Agarwal, Xu, and Poo, 2011, p. 1096). While the responses to these questions were collected as it pertained to a specific task or project that the survey participant would be engaged in at that point in time, the comfort level is subject to change over time, if there is a change in relationship between the actor and the source. The study found that lack of comfort with a source had a significant negative effect on the preference of use of the source and the amount of time a source is used, but not on the frequency of use. Actors seemed "to prefer to approach sources they are more comfortable with first and spend more time with them. Yet they use sources they are less comfortable with as frequently as other sources" (Agarwal, Xu, and Poo, 2011, p. 1110).

The actor-source relationship and notion of stereotyped context would relate to all domains. It has applications in specific types of information behavior, and in specific domains of information seeking behavior, e.g., in health information seeking. For instance, as we stereotype other people, we also have a stereotype of a physician. So, we select a particular physician as an information source or we do not, based on this stereotype (and depending on whether the source is part of our shared context or our stereotyped context). Similarly, physicians and medical residents select particular types of information sources based on the degree to which a source is part of their stereotyped context or shared context (e.g., see Agarwal et al. 2012). Thus, the notion of stereotyped context plays an important role in health information seeking, a specific domain of information behavior. Johnson and Case (2012) provide an in-depth review of health information seeking. Case and Given (2016) discuss the health information seeking behaviors of physicians, nurses, and other health care providers (pp. 295-304) and of patients (pp. 335–341).

Apart from applications in health information seeking, Chatman's research has delved into the insiders-outsiders small world model of information seeking, where disadvantaged groups called outsiders keep out insider information (see Chatman, 1996). This fits well with the notion of stereotyped context, and of the in-group/out-group distinction affected by the actor-source relationship, which influences whether an actor (Chatman's "outsider") places a particular source within a shared context or the stereotyped context.

Thus, the notion of stereotyped context and the actor's placement of sources between shared or stereotyped contexts for specific sources, and for the same source at different points in time, finds application in different areas of information seeking behavior, as well as in other aspects of information behavior such as serendipitous finding of information, information avoidance, information use, etc.

4.2.1   YIN-YANG: STEREOTYPING WITHIN SHARED VIEW OF CONTEXT

The Chinese principle of Yin and Yang is that all things exist as inseparable and contradictory opposites. "The ten thousand things carry [at their backs] the *yin* and embrace [in front] the *yang*; through the blending of the energy [chi] of these two, they achieve harmony." (Mitchell, 1998, p. 112) Thus, do the shared view of context and the stereotyped view of context balance each other? Is there a little bit of stereotyping in the shared view, and a little bit of shared context in the stereotyped view of context?

Figure 4.3: Yin-Yang: stereotyping within shared view of context; shared context within stereotyped view of context.

Stereotypes can be seen as understandings that we simplify or abstract in order to handle our world's complexity. In many types of interpersonal interactions, we stereotype another person or entity because dealing with all the particulars of those people and other entities that we interact with is not possible, due to the cognitive load it entails. For example, if I use a close friend as an information source for a particular question, it is relatively unlikely that I approach them because of my full nuanced understanding of them as a person. Instead, it is likely I approach them because they are an "expert" in the area of my information need. So I have stereotyped them, even though I know them well. We are both "insiders" and have a shared context, but stereotyping still happens. The same dynamics apply within teams or groups. If team members share a conception of the team's context, it is most likely that they are all just stereotyping elements of that context in similar ways. It is unlikely that no stereotyping is going on. Thus, stereotyping can be seen as a process of simplifying and abstracting aspects of the actors and entities relevant to a particular interaction. All human participants in the interaction can call on stereotyping as a tool for moving forward with the interaction.

Similarly, the stereotyping of actors and teams by positivist researchers, system developers, and others in the stereotyped view of context may not be absolute. There is likely to be elements of connectedness with the research subjects, participants, or end users. It is this harmony between the shared and stereotyped views of context allow people to straddle across these two ends of the continuum, or the opposing but balancing forces of Yin and Yang.

a. Role of Positivist vs. Interpretivist Researchers

I have chosen to include the Context Stereotype as a separate view in the Contextual Identity Framework because it captures the stereotyping role of positivist researchers. This argument is parallel to these researchers' goal of keeping the researcher out of view when data gathering. System developers also stereotype actors when they try to develop systems for the typical "user." Alternative approaches to research (such as those by an interpretivist or qualitative researcher) have no such goal and are explicitly oriented toward understanding an interaction from the perspective of the participants in the process, i.e., from the perspective/view of the individual actor or the members of the team. The personal view of context and the shared view of context will apply most to these researchers, while the stereotyped view will not be applicable to them. Interpretivist researchers may call on stereotyping as a tool for simplifying a study design, as necessary.

4.2.2   CONTEXTUAL IDENTITY FRAMEWORK AND SOCIAL PHENOMENOLOGY

In the Contextual Identity Framework (Section 3.2.4), we identified three views of context—(1) that of the actor (personal view); (2) of a team or group (shared view); and (3) of an outside researcher, a system designer, or another person (stereotyped view).

The idea of the personal view of context finds resonance with the concept of social phenomenology. This personal view is particularly subjective in nature just as phenomenological sociology, whose emphasis is on "understanding reality through the perspective of the acting subject rather than through the lens of the scientific observer" (Farganis, 2011, p. 257). Noted sociological phenomenologist Alfred Schütz, basing his thinking on the prior work of two philosophers Max Weber and Edmund Husserl, described the mundane happenings of the everyday life of people as their "life world" (Schütz, 1967; Schütz and Luckmann, 1973)—"an intersubjective world in which people both create social reality and are constrained by the preexisting social and cultural structures created by their predecessors" (Ritzer, 2011, p. 219). As per Schütz, this vast world (soziale Welt) forming our social experience "is constituted in an immensely complicated network of dimensions, relations, and modes of knowledge" (Walsh, 1967, p. xxvii, as writing in the introduction to Schütz, 1967). The context relating to an actor's information behavior would be the subset of such a world.

Schütz' theory of life world consists of four divisions.

1. The first comprises the world of immediate consociates or "fellow men" [or the more gender-neutral fellow persons] (social reality that the actor has directly experienced with people and artifacts who share with the actor a community of space and a community of time). Toward "a consociate I have what Schütz calls a 'Thou [or you] orientation' (Dueinstellung). If this is reciprocated, a face-to-face situation results, and we have a "We-relationship" (Wirbeziehung)" (Walsh, 1967, p. xxvii). This would equate to having a degree of shared context.

   Shared context accords with the notion of intersubjectivity explained by Schütz (Schütz and Luckmann, 1973). He writes that:

   "in the natural attitude of everyday life the following is taken for granted without question: (a) the corporeal existence of other [persons]; (b) that these bodies are endowed with consciousness essentially similar to my own; (c) that the things in the outer world included in my environs and that of my fellow-[persons] are the same for us and have fundamentally the same meaning; (d) that I can enter into interrelations and reciprocal actions with my fellow-[persons]; (e) that I can make myself understood to them (which follows from the preceding assumptions); (f) that a stratified social and cultural world is historically pre-given as a frame of reference to me and my fellow-[persons], indeed in a manner as taken for granted as the "natural world"; (g) that therefore the situation [context as situation] in which I find myself at any moment is only to a small extent purely created by me" (Schütz and Luckmann, 1973, p. 6).

   Schütz further explains that the:

   "everyday reality of the life-world includes…not only the 'nature' experienced by me but also the social (and therefore the cultural) world in which I find myself; the life-world is not

created out of the merely material objects and events which I encounter in my environment. Certainly, these are together one component of my surrounding world; nevertheless, there also belong to this all the meaning-strata which transform natural things into cultural objects, human bodies into fellow-men, and the movements of fellow-men into acts, gestures and communications" (Schütz and Luckmann, 1973, p. 6).

In this assigning of meaning that Schütz refers to above, there is an indication of the movement from stereotyped context to shared context.

The other three divisions in Schütz's life world comprise worlds that are not directly experienced by the actor but are on the horizon of direct experience. These include:

2. the world of contemporaries;

3. the world of predecessors; and

4. the world of successors.

The last two represent past and future (Walsh, 1967). While the (environmental) context of an actor during a particular information behavior is shaped by the context and behavior of predecessors, the actor's information behavior has the potential to shape the context and behavior of successors.

Contemporaries represent people who live during the same time, if not share the same space, and could move to the category of consociates (Walsh, 1967). Although they coexist with me in objective time, I can only comprehend them at a distance and by means of a peculiar inferential process. (Walsh, 1967, p. xxviii) "…We interpret the contemporaries…as being persons of such and such a type. In short, when interpreting the behavior of our contemporaries, we are resorting to *ideal types*" (Walsh, 1967, p. xxviii). Thus, the use of ideal types happens when we pass from direct to indirect social experience (Walsh, 1967). *Ideal types* are used in the process of stereotyping. Contemporaries, as per Schütz, can then be thought of as those information sources (people, books, systems, etc.) with which the actor has not had direct experience, and would fall in the realm of stereotyped context. As the actor starts getting to know a source, the degree of kinship increases, and the source moves toward shared context.

"My contemporaries are therefore something less than fully concrete persons for me. Their degree of concreteness may vary. My friend, whom I saw last week and who has just sent me a letter, is almost as concrete to me as if he were present in person. But the postal clerk who will cancel my letter and whose existence I merely assume when I drop the letter in the box is almost completely 'anonymous'. With a contemporary we can have only a relationship at a distance, a They-relationship, based on a corresponding relatively abstract They-orientation, which is in turn made possible by the use of ideal types" (Walsh, 1967, p. xxviii).

People with whom an actor has been friends, for instance only on Facebook or through messaging, may be included in the actor's world of consociates, as there could be a degree of kinship or closeness even though only virtual space is shared, and not physical. These actor-source relationships (actor-actor relationships if the source is a person) would be stronger than those with contemporaries, but weaker than those people that the actor has known and spent time with in person.

> *"Ideal types [sources in an actor's stereotyped context] can be arranged on a scale of increasing anonymity. There is, for instance, my absent friend, his brother whom he has described to me, the professor whose books I have read, the postal clerk, the Canadian Parliament, abstract entities like Canada itself, the rules of English grammar, or the basic principles of jurisprudence. As the types get more and more abstract, we are…getting further and further away from the actual subjective meaning-complexes or contexts of individuals [the personal view of context]. We are making more and more use of objective contexts of meaning [the stereotyped view of context]. But these refer by their very nature to subjective meaning-contexts of greater or lesser anonymity"* (Walsh, 1967, p. xxviii).

Thus, the stereotyped view of context (as seen by an outside researcher) is referring to the personal and shared view of context (as experienced by an actor or a team).

"We have at last arrived at the answer to the crucial question 'What is social science?' Social science, Schütz replies, is an objective context of meaning constructed out of and referring to subjective contexts of meaning" (Walsh, 1967, p. xxviii). Inferring from this definition, we can define social science as a stereotyped view of context constructed out of and referring to personal and shared views of context. Thus, the stereotyped view of context (Figures 3.5 and 3.11) is very close to the definition of social science as per Schütz.

> *"The fundamental tool of social science is, as Weber claimed, the ideal type. Although the ideal type is present in all cases of indirect understanding of another person, it has a special function in social science. It must be fitted into a whole hierarchy of other objective concepts making up the total complex of scientific knowledge"* (Walsh, 1967, pp. xxviii–xxix).

As we noted earlier in Table 3.2, the stereotyped view of context is a convenient simplification which is not reflective of actual reality (a research imperative; important for design of search systems). Here, the ideal types (the result of intergroup behavior as per Figure 3.2) play a prominent role in simplifying and making sense of reality (though they don't reflect the reality of the individual actor who just happens to be a member of the group that the researcher is interested in studying). Studies which see "context as environment or container" (e.g., Rieh, 2004; Lamb, King, and Kling, 2003) can be seen to reduce the actor to this ideal type. Researchers such as Dervin (1997) and Dourish (2004) have criticized this view as being devoid of reality. However, the stereotyped view of context is an outcome of this natural categorization process of human cognition, which looks for ideal types to make sense of the world.

Thus, while all context is subjective and dynamic (as denoted by the personal view of context and the shared view of context) and can be bounded only insofar as it exists in the mind of a particular actor at a particular point in time, positivist researchers and designers of information systems for search may nevertheless attempt to objectify this subjective context (much like the definition of social science provided by Schütz, 1967). In the tables in Section 2.2.3 and in Table 3.4, we had italicized the more stables parts of context in information behavior—primarily relating to the actor and the source/system/channel, as well as some other variables from other elements. Researchers and designers can decide whether to only include the more dynamic variables that change from situation to situation (those not italicized), or include variables from the more stable parts of context as well.

We can link the attempt at objectifying a subjective context to the process of stereotyping (Tajfel and Turner, 1979). This attempt is crucial because it paves the path for designing search systems that could be applicable in various settings such as organizations, home environment, etc. However, to be truly effective, these systems must be designed keeping in mind that context (from the point of view of the actor) is actually subjective in nature, and the actor must have room to modify the search system as per his/her unique set of requirements at a particular point in time. The interpretive researcher often studies this subjective context.

Let us now discuss how context can overlap and how it is subject to continuous reshaping and change.

4.3 CONTEXT OVERLAP AND CONTINUOUS CHANGE

In the Contextual Identity Framework (Section 3.2.4), we saw that each view of context has the levels of personal context, shared context and stereotyped context. Let us briefly investigate the relationship between these levels, using the personal view of context (Figure 3.3) for discussion. Some of the discussion in the following sections is adapted from Agarwal, Xu, and Poo (2009).

4.3.1 LAYERS OF CONTEXT OR OVERLAPPING CONTEXTS

In an organizational context, environmental variables such as work role, corporate culture, norms, etc. are part of the actor's shared context (Table 3.4). When seen from the actor's point of view (in the personal view of context), the level of personal context (comprising actor variables such as the actor's thoughts and feelings, personality, etc.) is generally the strongest. The shared context of work role/team is expected to be more cohesive and stronger than organizational factors such as corporate culture, norms and resources (see Figure 4.4). These, in turn, are expected to have a stronger influence than factors outside the organization. As we move from the innermost circle of personal context to the outer circles with lesser degrees of cohesiveness, the degree of anonymity can be expected to increase (as per the life world theory of Schütz, 1967; Schütz and Luckmann, 1973). As the degree of anonymity increases, an increasing amount of stereotyping might take place. Apart from my earlier work in Agarwal, Xu, and Poo (2009), nested contexts are also shown in Kari and Savolainen (2003), Sonnenwald (1999), Williamson (1998), and Wilson (1981). An important milestone in the history of nested views is found in Paisley (1968), in which he discusses an actor (as scientist) seeing the world through a series of concentric circles, starting with "within his own head" and ending with "within his culture."

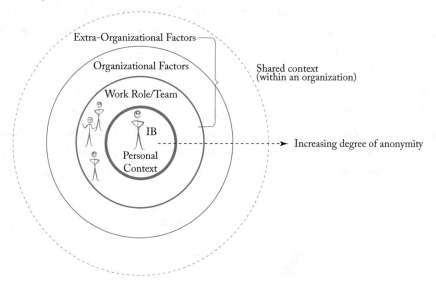

Figure 4.4: Concentric circles of shared context within an organization—personal view of context (adapted from Agarwal, Xu, and Poo, 2009).

As Ingwersen and Järvelin (2005) point out, taking context in isolation doesn't work. "In IS&R [information seeking and retrieval], *actors* and other components function as context to one another in the interaction processes. There are social, organizational, cultural as well as systemic contexts, which evolve over time" (p. 19; author's italics). "All IS&R components and activities are in context of common social, physical and technological infrastructures as well as their history over time" (p. 383). The place of context in most of systems-oriented information retrieval (IR) research has been similar to the 'context-as-container or environment' view (the stereotyped view of context). However, in cognitive and user-oriented research, "IR is placed in context in a holistic way: all components/cognitive actors and structures of IS&R are contextual to one another" (Ingwersen and Järvelin, 2005, p. 193).

4.3.2 CONTINUOUS RESHAPING OF CONTEXT

In the Contextual Identity Framework—as seen by the actor in the personal view of context (and shared view of context)—the three levels of context do not operate in isolation. Rather, the different levels coexist and work in tandem. For example, factors such as the searcher's individual habits and commitment to professional development might be personal contextual factors, but are subject to influence by shared contextual factors such as corporate culture, availability of information systems and sources, etc. While in Figure 4.4, I have shown the personal context to be strongest, how strong or weak a particular view is might be subject to cultural influence. A person adhering to an individualistic culture (see Hofstede, 1980) might give more importance to personal context than shared context. Conversely, a person adhering to a collectivistic culture (Hofstede, 1980) might give more importance to shared context than personal context. This is represented by the shared view of context (Figure 3.4), where the shared circle of the team or group context may be stronger than that of personal context, depending on culture and the individuals involved in the team.

An actor's context is continuously shaped through the interaction of the external environment (which is seen as objective and external, and either at the level of the stereotyped or the shared context, depending on the degree of kinship the actor feels with specific people, artifacts, systems or processes in the environment) and the way the actor perceives it to be (subjective, internal—personal or shared context) (see Figure 4.5). The three levels of context (in a particular view of context) continuously shape each other.

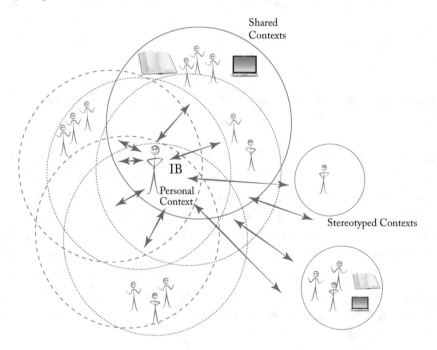

Figure 4.5: Continuous shaping of context through the interaction of factors external to the actor and the actor's perception of those factors (adapted from Agarwal, Xu, and Poo, 2009).

There might also be conflicts between the different circles of an actor's shared context, which affect the actor's information behavior at different points in time. As Sonnenwald (1999) writes, contexts "are not discrete entities; two or more contexts may share common attributes. For example, a faculty member may be a teacher, researcher and administrator. From an outsider's perspective, it may be difficult to determine when the faculty [member]'s behavior is attributable to the context of teaching, research or administration. An individual may concurrently try to satisfy constraints of different contexts, e.g., as happens when a parent brings children to the office when no other child-care options exist for them. We often learn more about contexts when conflicts among contexts emerge" (p. 179).

Since the contextual elements relating to the actor, the environment, the task or situation, the need, the source or channel, the actor-source relationship and time/space interact in unique ways for an actor engaged in information behavior at any point in time and space, the perception of each individual in the world then becomes unique. Thus, since contexts overlap in different ways, each person becomes unique. Your overlapping contexts make you different from anyone else. That is what makes stereotyping a futile exercise in trying to know a person, "because no person is the average of his/her culture...we fight as human beings to fall in line. We fight as human beings to fall out of line" (Dervin, 2011, 28:21-28:29; Agarwal, 2012). This jostle to stay in line and fall out of line is a reflection of the continuous shaping of the actor's context, as seen in Figure 4.5.

My personal take is that people are like rivers—constantly flowing, as we ourselves are. Each experience at every moment in time shapes us and changes us, even though we (as well as other people) appear to be mostly the same. When we meet a person and make a judgment, we are essentially taking a snapshot of a flowing river. The person, as well as us, would have moved forward since then. Thus, the act of knowing someone is a misnomer—rather, we can say we know someone as the person was at that particular point in time, or at the moments when we interacted with the person. Due to the ephemeral nature of the interaction, we might, thus, be stereotyping more often than we realize—of at least some aspects of the context surrounding our interaction with that person.

Table 4.1 summarizes the discussion above on layers of context, and changes in context (as seen from a particular view of context).

Table 4.1: Layers of context and changes in context (in particular views of context)			
Level	**Personal context**	**Shared context**	**Stereotyped context**
Layers of context	Multiple layers of context; some strong, some weak	A few layers of largely simple contexts; 1–2 layers of shared context may be stronger than the rest	Context outside one's personal boundaries of context; perception based on biases or anonymity
Degree of change	Few factors are largely static (e.g., sex or ethnicity), with more dynamic boundaries based on activity	Largely static boundaries for some group memberships, and dynamic for the others, especially when joining new groups or leaving existing ones	Dynamic boundaries often ignored in favour of one fixed, static boundary used as a judging lens

4.4   CHAPTER SUMMARY

In this chapter, we discussed how the framework of context elements and variables can be applied in the design of research studies in information behavior. We also examined why stereotyped context is important and how an actor might decide to place a context element within the circles of shared or stereotyped context. We explored context in relation to social phenomenology, and how context overlaps and reshapes continuously. With the empirical literature review and the conceptual background in place, we will now attempt to arrive at a unified definition of context in information behavior.

CHAPTER 5

Definition and Conclusions

We set out to examine the differing conceptual understandings of context, and the contextual elements identified in the many empirical studies on context in information behavior. With that foundation, we started answering the following questions. What does context really mean? How do we map the conceptual space of context? What are the boundaries of context? What are the variables that make up context in information behavior and that can be incorporated into research studies? Finally, in the last chapter, we saw how we can design research studies incorporating context and how the boundaries of context move and reshape.

Now, we will arrive at a unified definition of context in information behavior. We will also look at limitations and future work, and conclusions and implications. Finally, we will look at the role of context in information behavior in the near future.

5.1   TOWARD A UNIFIED DEFINITION OF "CONTEXT IN INFORMATION BEHAVIOR"

Based on our literature review and the Contextual Identity Framework, we can arrive at a few conclusions about context.

1. Context is of an entity with respect to a behavior or activity. Here, the entity in question is the actor engaged in any information behavior, which can include information seeking, information searching and retrieval, interaction with a person or device, serendipitous finding, collaborative information behavior, information sharing, information use, information avoiding, etc. Without the behavior or activity (where the state of rest or inactivity can also be a behavior), context doesn't have much meaning or use. The same person would have a different set of contexts at different points of conversation, behavior and interaction. As Dourish (2004) writes, context is always created at the point of interaction (although we could define interaction more broadly than just interaction with a computer/device, which the field of human-computer interaction is concerned with; we can understand it based on the actor's interaction with information (provided by a source through a channel). Thus, context is of the actor engaged in an activity at the point of interaction.

2. Context is always about relationship—of an actor with elements outside of the actor (people, artifacts, processes, situations, environment) or even of the actor with themselves (depending on who's watching) e.g., actor with respect to the task, actor

w.r.t. the situation at hand, actor w.r.t. work colleagues, actor w.r.t. the actor. These elements, in themselves, do not form the context (except as they are related to the actor, or any other entity in question).

3. Context is not one "whole" concept, which will look the same from every direction. Depending on who you are, where you're looking from, and who the actor in question in, context will appear differently to you. There are three views of context—the actor's personal view of context, the shared view of context, and a stereotyped view of context. The first two views may be most used by the interpretivist researcher. The positivist researcher and the system developer may be using the third, stereotyped view.

4. For an actor looking at one's own context, everything will appear as context (the actor's personal context such as thoughts, feelings, identity, abilities, etc.; the shared context of the actor as a part of groupings based on age, gender, ethnicity, religion, region, country, education, job focus, etc.—those that the actor considers "in-group"; and the stereotyped contexts of the actor—people and artifacts that the actor is not familiar with, or chooses not to identify with. However, an interpretive researcher studying the actor in one's own context might decide to focus more on the dynamic aspects of the context, and may or may not choose to include the more stable attributes relating to the actor, source, and other elements (italicized in the tables in Section 2.2.3 and in Table 3.4).

5. For an actor looking at one's own context with a friend, colleague or collaborator (part of a shared group), context includes the personal contexts of the two actors—individual thoughts, feelings, abilities, etc.; the shared context (common ground, history of working together, common worldview, shared physical space, shared resources, etc.); and the individually or collectively stereotyped contexts of the two actors (people and artifacts that the one or more actors are not familiar with, or choose not to identify with). Here, too, the interpretivist researcher may choose to focus more on those context attributes that are likely to change across situations (the ones not italicized in the tables in Section 2.2.3 and in Table 3.4), and, optionally, decide to include some more stable attributes of the seeker, source/system/channel and other elements.

6. For a positivist researcher or system designer looking at a participant's or user's context, context will be everything that surrounds the actor (such as the physical setting, the environment, people/colleagues, computers, artifacts, books, etc.), but does not include the actor. More than simply surrounding, Lee (2011) stresses on the importance of entities being related to the actor. He defines context as a "set of

things, factors, elements and attributes that are related to a target entity in important ways (e.g., operationally, semantically, conceptually or pragmatically) but are not so closely related to the target entity that they are considered to be exclusively part of the target entity itself" (p. 96). Thus, a researcher may choose to not see the more stable attributes of actors—and of sources/systems/channels—(italicized in the tables in Section 2.2.3 and in Table 3.4) as part of the context of an interaction.

7. The elements of the context of an actor engaged in an activity (information behavior/ interaction) include aspects of the environment, the task or problem situation, the need or information required, the actor and his/her/their identity, the source/system/ channel, the actor-source relationship, and time/space.

8. The relationships among the elements of and the different views of context can be understood via properties, which "help to perceive the central structures and regularity", and to "underline dynamism between the modular descriptions of context." They "condense the differences in the examination levels within components of context" (Jumisko-Pyykkö and Vainio, 2010, p. 13).

9. The elements of context can differ based on the level of magnitude, ranging from micro to the macro (Jumisko-Pyykkö and Vainio, 2010). This property pertains to the lens of viewing context, where a nearby element, e.g., a cup of coffee, a book one is reading, etc. would be part of the micro context, and an element far away, e.g., the government, a neighbor, the next street, etc. would be macro.

10. The different elements of context during the course of an interaction would differ based on their level of dynamism, ranging from the static to the dynamic (Jumisko-Pyykkö and Vainio, 2010). The things that remain mostly constant over time (e.g., one's office space, time of browsing, etc.) are static, while things that change, e.g., the webpage one is reading, are dynamic. The attributes of elements that I have italicized in the tables in Section 2.2.3 and in Table 3.4 are the more static ones.

11. Elements of context may be repetitive or non-repetitive, i.e., may follow a pattern ranging from rhythmic to random; "something that happens just once" or is an exception "to the common form of use" (Jumisko-Pyykkö and Vainio, 2010, p. 14). For example, the actor might use the Facebook app on a smartphone on a regular basis, but use another app infrequently. A person in an office job would have a more regular surrounding context, as opposed to a traveling salesman.

12. There can be numerous combinations between different elements of context, many of which co-occur on a frequent or regular basis in an actor's information behavior.

The actor might need to respond to a situation on a regular basis, e.g., a student needing to answer the queries raised by the professor in the same classroom, and at the same time of the day during the semester.

Based on these 12 conclusions above, we can arrive at the following inferences about context: The context of an actor's information behavior includes aspects of the environment, the task, the need, the actor, the source or the system, the relationship between the actor and the source, and time and space that are relevant to the behavior. An actor or social group engaged in a behavior will see context differently than others, both of whom will make an in-group/out-group differentiation of elements of the context depending on one's individual and shared identities. Elements and different views of context relate to and differ from each other depending on the level of magnitude, the level of dynamism, and the pattern of occurrence, and co-occur in different combinations.

Based on these inferences, we arrive at the following definition of context: *"The context of an actor's information behavior consists of elements such as environment, task, actor-source relationship, time, etc. that are relevant to the behavior during the course of interaction and vary based on magnitude, dynamism, patterns and combinations, and that appear differently to the actor than to others, who make an in-group/out-group differentiation of these elements depending on their individual and shared identities."*

Having arrived at the unified definition of context, let us briefly discuss the limitations of the work.

5.2   LIMITATIONS AND FUTURE WORK

In this book, I have attempted to map the concept of context in information behavior through a review of the literature, a series of frameworks and a definition of context. However, it has a few limitations.

First, I have investigated context largely from an information science perspective as it pertains to information behavior. We have discussed the literature on human-computer interaction (HCI) and the way context applies to mobile information behavior, but not as the central focus of the book. Future work can focus on context in mobile information behavior, and the way it applies to the HCI community. Such a work as a follow up to this book project can also serve as a bridge between the information behavior and HCI communities. Researchers can also investigate how other fields have applied context. For example, Lamsfus et al. (2015) discuss context-aware system design with the aim of defining the notion of context as it relates to the mobile technological environment for tourism.

Second, I have based a large number of studies and frameworks (as well as discussion in this book) on an actor's information seeking behavior when faced with a task or situation that requires looking for information. However, there are other aspects of information behavior where context plays a major role, e.g., in serendipitous information encountering, information capture and creation, information use, as well as in information avoidance and information stopping behavior. While I have included these, and discussed them in places, they have not received the same coverage as information seeking. The frameworks of contextual elements and variables should, however, apply to different forms of information behavior, and to the study of this behavior within specific domains such as healthcare, universities, libraries, government, etc. Future studies should investigate context within other specific forms of information behavior, and highlight any differences that need to be taken into account. Studies should also look at the effect of context on information practices, as distinct from information behavior (discussed in Section 2.2.3, under the sub-section "other information behavior and practices affected by context"). The shared view of context would especially be applicable to information practices. The relationship between the two should be explored further.

Third, the frameworks arrived at (Contextual Identity Framework, framework of context elements, and framework of context variables) need to be tested in the design and conduct of future empirical studies. While a few studies, e.g., Agarwal, Xu, and Poo (2011), were discussed, more research needs to be conducted where these frameworks are used as a base for study design. Other researchers can also test the frameworks by mapping them to past studies (see Chapter 2, as well as Case and Given, 2016). This would help determine if there are other contextual variables or elements that need to have a place in the framework. Fourth, the list of variables (in Figure 3.11 and Table 3.4), while long, may not be completely exhaustive. It is always possible to label a social science construct in different ways. There could be more variables that would easily apply to a particular element of context. Future researchers should identity variables that are missing and add to the framework and table. Also, researchers might be able to find interesting interactions (mediating and moderating effects) between specific contextual variables in the framework.

Fifth, the frameworks need to be tested by system designers to see the extent to which they help in the design of search systems that keep the actor or the user (and the actor's personal context) as the central focus. We had discussed context in the design of systems in Section 2.2.4. I will discuss the future implications of context briefly in the last section.

Next, the literature review could be made even more exhaustive to include treatments of context in other related areas apart from information retrieval. Finally, the unified definition of context in information behavior could potentially be shortened.

5.3   CONCLUSIONS AND IMPLICATIONS

In this book, I have attempted to do a few things. I have tried to bring together the many definitions of context, and the labels that researchers have used to refer to context. We have looked at different models and frameworks in information behavior, and how researchers have applied context in those. Next, we identified various contextual elements, populations, and research methods used from a detailed literature review of studies in information behavior. We then sought to delineate the boundaries of context using the Contextual Identity Framework.

One of the relatively novel contributions of this book is in the incorporation of social identity theory as a frame for conceptualizing context. The main point of the theory (useful for our purposes) is that an actor has an individual identity and also has one or more social identities, shaped by the group(s) in which the actor participates. The influence of the group on the individual actor's information behavior may be stronger or weaker, depending on the relationship between the individual and the group and how that relationship pertains to the situation at hand. By distinguishing an individual view of context from a shared view of context, this book will help to incorporate social influences into our considerations of context.

A central contribution of the framework is the understanding that context will appear different depending on who is viewing it—whether an individual actor, a team or collective (and those immersed in shared contexts of the individual or collective), or someone observing a person or group from afar. Within each view, there is the level of the individual, of the social group, and of people and artifacts outside the shared circles, which help explain the different layers of context. These layers interact with each other, affect each other, and are shaped and reshaped continuously. Specific elements and variables can be applied to elements within these different levels and layers of context.

Another contribution is recognizing the importance of the stereotyped view of context in the design of quantitative research studies and in system design. In explaining the problem of inter-subjective understanding, Alfred Schutz distinguishes between "the genuine understanding of the other person and the abstract conceptualization of [the person's] actions or thoughts as being of such and such type...Merely to understand the general kind of action in which another is engaging is merely to order one's own experiences into categories, or what Schutz calls "self-elucidation" (Selbstauslegung)" (Walsh, 1967, p. xxv; Schütz, 1967). Can researchers and system designers go beyond self-elucidation? While a researcher or a designer cannot "directly intuit another person's subjective experiences" (Walsh, 1967, p. xxv; Schütz, 1967), Schütz stresses the importance of si-multaneity, where we "sense that the other person's stream of consciousness is flowing along a track that is temporally parallel with our own" (Walsh, 1967, p. xxv). Is it necessary for a designer to ste-reotype in order to design a system that will work well for more than one actor/group? Is it possible for the researcher and the subject, or the designer and the user, to reach this perfect synchronicity suggested by Walsh where the designer does not just assume but genuinely helps the user figure out their needs? Researchers using interpretivist and mixed method approaches have an opportunity here, where they can study subjective assessments of a particular context.

The definition of context arrived at synthesizes the various understandings about context arrived at thus far by a series of researchers. The unified definition might help us move forward into the future with a common understanding, rather than having to reinvent the wheel at every turn.

5.4   CONTEXT NOW AND IN THE NEAR FUTURE

I want to leave you with a few thoughts on the role of context in our current world and the near future.

Context when physical and digital boundaries are blurring

We are living in a world where the boundary between the physical and the digital worlds is increasingly blurred. People are increasingly torn between the physical and digital contexts. People tend to say, "You should turn off your phones, and be 'more present' in the here and now," where here and now means physical. Should you be more present in the digital here and now, or not? In which case, should you be carrying smartphones at all? And if you do, does your presence only mean physical presence, or also a response to the likes you received to a post or to a picture you posted 30 minutes ago? Thus, it may not just be enough to be talking about the physical here and now in a world connected with and led by smartphone, email, messaging and other forms of smartphone-and-tablet-mediated communication. You are still experiencing real life, because you are still interacting with other humans. Rather than concentrating on physical vs. the virtual, context as place can be better understood mostly as a cognitive or a mental state, i.e., what occupies your mind at a given time. It could be your physical environment, a virtual interaction, a book you are reading, a painting you are making, or an online webinar you are giving. It is your experience of immersion that matters most—like a task or situation that occupies your mind.

Loss of context as undesirable

There are people who communicate mostly (or sometimes only) through messaging. With the inherent limitations of these media, a "poor context" is communicated to one party to the conversation. We need to find new, sane ways of communicating in today's world—where an understanding of context becomes crucial. System designers need to find solutions to communicate context more effectively and seamlessly in such scenarios, apart from automated messages like "[I am currently] in a meeting", etc.

Loss of context as desirable

It might be important to have the ability to disconnect from context; e.g., there is a traffic jam and you are late for work, but since there is nothing you can do, you email your boss or your colleague, and then decide to enjoy the surroundings, and count the different types, colors and makes of cars on the road. If the physical environment is stressful, then people can use the help of the digital world to get into a different context, and disconnect from the physical stress.

Context as an interplay between the stable and the transient

Context is an interplay between the "here and now", the details, the transient, everyday parts, vs. the more stable parts of our environment and who we are (our personalities, behavioral traits, philosophical and spiritual sides, etc.). How important is it to pay attention to something fleeting and transient—the changing context? Can we really keep up with the changing contexts of 500 or more (sometimes 5,000) of our Facebook friends in a digitally connected world? Or should we be more worried about the more unchanging part? One reason why SnapChat has succeeded as an app is that it does not store, incorporates the transient and the mundane, and helps people feel connected. The informal and the transient may be the more important parts of our context in everyday lives, and could inform varied fields from interpersonal communication to knowledge management to happiness.

The changing context

Our physical context can change as we carry our phone from our house to the road and then to an office. Similarly, the digital context can change as we are in an online meeting, where another person joins in, or when we receive an email notification in the middle of a phone conversation. Thus, context can quickly become confusing.

5.5   CHAPTER SUMMARY

In this chapter, we arrived at 12 conclusions about context, which gave rise to this unified definition: "The context of an actor's information behavior consists of elements such as environment, task, actor, source, time, etc. that are relevant to the behavior at the point of interaction and vary based on magnitude, dynamism, patterns and combinations, and that appear differently to the actor than to others, who make an in-group/out-group differentiation of these elements depending on their individual and shared identities."

We then looked at conclusions and implications, and some of my thoughts on the role of context in today's world. Actors sometimes stay (cognitively) in the physical, sometimes the digital, and sometimes seamlessly straddle the physical and digital worlds. Our understanding of context, work, lifestyle, and system design must all be informed by this ease of movement between the different worlds, and the support mechanisms that need to be provided (in different elements of context) to facilitate such movement by the actor. Can we redesign contexts to make people happier?

CHAPTER 6

Further Reading

A number of books and research articles in journals and conference proceedings are important in continuing to keep abreast with research in context in information behavior.

- *Proceedings of Information Seeking in Context (ISIC)*, the Information Behavior Conference

- *Proceedings of the ACM SIGIR Conference on Human Information Interaction and Retrieval (CHIIR)*. The conference was previously called IIiX (Symposia on Information Interaction in Context)

- *Proceedings of the Annual Meeting of the Association for Information Science and Technology* (the association was earlier called the American Society for Information Science and Technology)

- *Journal of the Association for Information Science and Technology (JASIS&T)*

- *Looking for Information: A Survey of Research on Information Seeking, Needs, and Behavior* (Fourth Edition) by Case and Given (2016) (the first three editions of the book were single-authored by Donald Case)

- Other information science journals

For articles on context in system design, and context-aware computing, see the following journals, conference proceedings and book:

- *ACM Transactions on Computer Human Interaction (TOCHI)*

- *Behavior and Information Technology*

- *International Journal of Human-Computer Studies*

- *Human-Computer Interaction*

- *Personal and Ubiquitous Computing (PUC)*

- *Proceedings of the SIGCHI Conference on Human Factors in Computing Systems (CHI)*

- *Mobile Learning: The Next Generation* by Traxler and Kukulska-Hulme (2016), which includes discussions on technologies and applications for context-aware mobile learning in various settings.

The following are examples of useful articles on context (listed chronologically by year):

- *Toward a Better Understanding of Context and Context-Awareness* by Abowd, Dey, Brown, Davies, Smith, and Steggles (1999)

- *A Survey of Context-aware Mobile Computing Research* by Chen and Kotz (2000)

- *Understanding and Using Context* by Dey (2001)

- *What We Talk About When We Talk About Context* by Dourish (2004)

- *Context in Information Behavior Research* by Courtright (2007)

- *An Operational Definition of Context* by Zimmermann, Lorenz, and Oppermann (2007).

For other treatments of context see:

- *Proceedings of CONTEXT: The International and Interdisciplinary Conference on Modeling and Using Context.* Held every two years since 1999 (with the exception of 2009), the 10th conference was held in 2017. The conference accepts research in different disciplines related to issues of context and contextual knowledge.

- *Rethinking Context: Language as an Interactive Phenomenon* by Duranti and Goodwin (1992). This book looks at context in language use

- *Understanding Context: Environment, Language, and Information Architecture* by Hinton (2014). This book is targeted toward information architects, user experience professionals, and web and app designers.

Bibliography

Abad-Garcia, M., Gonzalez-Teruel, A., and Sanjuan-Nebot, L. (1999). Information needs of physicians at the University Clinic Hospital in Valencia, Spain. In T.D. Wilson and D.K. Allen (Eds.), *Exploring the Contexts of Information Behavior: Proceedings of the International Conference on Research in Information Needs, Seeking and Use in Different Contexts* (Sheffield, UK, Aug. 13–15, 1998) (pp. 209–225). London: Taylor Graham. 36, 38, 40, 46, 47, 55, 58, 59, 61, 68, 69, 70, 71

Abowd, G., Dey, A., Brown, P., Davies, N., Smith, M., and Steggles, P. (1999). Toward a better understanding of context and context-awareness. In *Handheld and Ubiquitous Computing* (pp. 304–307). Springer Berlin/Heidelberg. DOI: 10.1007/3-540-48157-5_29. 78, 134

Abrahamson, J. A., Fisher, K. E., Turner, A. G., Durrance, J. C., and Turner, T. C. (2008). Lay information mediary behavior uncovered: exploring how nonprofessionals seek health information for themselves and others online. *Journal of the Medical Library Association: JMLA*, 96(4), 310. 10

ACM Digital Library (2017). Conferences - IIiX Information Interaction in Context Symposium. Retrieved from http://dl.acm.org/event.cfm?id=RE296. 43

Agarwal, N. K. and Rahim, N. F.A. (2014). Student expectations from a cross-cultural virtual collaboration: A qualitative analysis. *QQML Journal*, 3(1), 221–234. 70, 71

Agarwal, N. K. (2009a). Information seeking behavior and context: Theoretical frameworks and an empirical study of source use (Doctoral dissertation). ScholarBank@NUS (Open Ph.D. Theses 6523) Retrieved from http://www.scholarbank.nus.edu.sg/handle/10635/16864. 8, 62, 63, 66, 110

Agarwal, N. K. (2009b). Use of technology to assert identity: Toward a theory of expanding circles of identity. *10th APRU Doctoral Students Conference*, Kyoto, Japan, Jul. 6–10. 85, 87

Agarwal, N. K. (2011). Information source and its relationship with the context of information seeking behavior. In *Proceedings of iConference 2011*, Seattle, WA, Feb. 8-11 (pp. 48–55). New York: ACM Digital Library. DOI: 10.1145/1940761.1940768. 1, 12, 19, 46, 67, 68, 69, 101, 103, 110

Agarwal, N. K. (2012). Making sense of sense-making: tracing the history and development of Dervin's sense-making methodology. In T. Carbo and T.B. Hahn (Eds.), *International*

Perspectives on the History of Information Science and Technology: Proceedings of the ASIS&T 2012 Pre-Conference on the History of ASIS&T and Information Science and Technology. (pp. 61–73). Medford, NJ: Information Today. 3, 5, 28, 87, 123

Agarwal, N.K. (2014). Use of touch devices by toddlers and preschoolers: Observations and findings from a single-case study. In Bilal, D. and Beheshti, J. (Eds.) *New Directions in Children and Adolescents' Information Behavior Research* (pp. 3–38), Library and Information Science, 10, Emerald Group publishing Limited. DOI: 10.1108/S1876-056220140000010045. 37, 39, 40, 44, 45, 52, 53, 56, 58, 63, 66, 67, 69

Agarwal, N. K. (2015). Toward a definition of serendipity in information behaviour. *Information Research*, 20(3), paper 675. Retrieved from http://InformationR.net/ir/20-3/pape675.html. 3, 4, 58, 59, 60, 61

Agarwal, N. K., Xu, Y. (C.), and Poo, D.C.C. (2011). A context-based investigation into source use by information seekers. *Journal of the American Society for Information Science and Technology*, 62(6), 1087–1104. DOI: 10.1002/asi.21513. 1, 11, 13, 19, 46, 47, 56, 58, 59, 61, 64, 65, 66, 67, 68, 69, 70, 71, 78, 101, 110, 111, 112, 114, 129

Agarwal, N. K., Xu, Y.(C.), and Poo, D.C.C. (2009). Delineating the boundary of 'context' in information behavior: Toward a contextual identity framework. *ASIS&T 2009 Annual Meeting* (Vancouver, Canada, Nov. 6–11). DOI: 10.1002/meet.2009.1450460252. 7, 8, 41, 81, 84, 87, 93, 120, 121, 122

Agarwal, N. K., Xu, Y.(C.), Lawrence, H., and Agarwal, A. (2012). Effect of institutional factors on source and channel use by medical residents. *Proceedings of the American Society for Information Science and Technology (ASIS&T 2012 Annual Meeting)* (Baltimore, MD, Oct. 26–30), 49–1, 1–4. DOI: 10.1002/meet.14504901364. 68, 69, 114

Algon, J. (1997). Classifications of tasks, steps, and information-related behaviors of individuals on project terms. In P. Vakkari, R. Savolainen, and B. Dervin (Eds.), *Information Seeking in Context: Proceedings of an International Conference on Research in Information Needs, Seeking and Use in Different Contexts* (Tampere, Finland, Aug. 14–16, 1996) (pp. 205–221). London: Taylor Graham. 36, 39, 40, 48, 49, 50, 54, 57, 58

Allen, B. (1996). *Information Tasks Toward a User-Centered Approach to Information Systems.* Academic Press. 72

Allen, B. (1997). Information needs: A person-in-situation approach. In P. Vakkari, R. Savolainen and B. Dervin (Eds.), *Information Seeking in Context: Proceedings of an International Conference on Research in Information Needs, Seeking and Use in Different Contexts* (Tampere, Finland, Aug. 14–16, 1996) (pp. 111–122). London: Taylor Graham. 10, 13

Allen, B. L. (2000). Individual differences and the conundrums of user centered design: Two experiments. *Journal of the American Society for Information Science*, 51(6), 508–520. DOI: 10.1002/(SICI)1097-4571(2000)51:6<508::AID-ASI3>3.0.CO;2-Q. 63

Allen, B. L. and Kim, K. -S. (2000). Person and context in information seeking: Interactions between cognitive and task variables. Proceedings of *ISIC 2000: Information Seeking in Context: The 3rd International Conference on Information Needs, Seeking and Use in Different Contexts* (Gothenburg, Sweden, Aug. 16-18, 2000). 9, 11

Allen, D. and Wilson, T. D. (2003). Information overload: context and causes. *The New Review of Information Behaviour Research*, 4(1), 31–44. DOI: 10.1080/14716310310001631426. 36, 38, 40, 48, 49, 50, 52, 53

Allen, D., Karanasios, S., and Slavova, M. (2011). Working with activity theory: Context, technology, and information behavior. *Journal of the American Society for Information Science and Technology*, 62(4), 776–788. DOI: 10.1002/asi.21441. 7, 18

Anderson, T. D. (2005). Relevance as process: judgements in the context of scholarly research. *Information Research*, 10(2), paper 226. Retrieved from http://informationr.net/ir/10-2/paper226.html. 36, 39, 40, 42, 55, 58, 64, 66, 70, 71, 112

Ariely, D. (2008). *Predictably Irrational: The Hidden Forces that Shape our Decisions.* New York: HarperCollins. 65

Ark, W. and Selker, T. (1999). A look at human interaction with pervasive computers. *IBM Systems Journal*, 38(4), 504–507. DOI: 10.1147/sj.384.0504. 72

Ashford, S. J. (1986). Feedback-seeking in individual adaptation: a resource perspective. *Academy of Management Journal*, 29, 465–487. DOI: 10.2307/256219. 70, 71

Askola, K., Atsushi, T. and Huotari, M-L. (2010). Cultural differences in the health information environments and practices between Finnish and Japanese university students. *Information Research*, 15(4), paper 451. Retrieved from http://www.informationr.net/ir/15-4/paper451.html. 36, 37, 40, 48, 49, 50, 52, 53

Bailey, E. and Kelly, D. (2016). Developing a measure of search expertise. In *Proceedings of the 2016 ACM Conference on Human Information Interaction and Retrieval* (pp. 237–240). ACM. DOI: 10.1145/2854946.2854983. 36, 38, 40, 44, 45, 64, 65, 66, 67

Barry, C. (1997). Information-seeking in an advanced IT culture: a case study. In P. Vakkari, R. Savolainen, and B. Dervin (Eds.), *Information Seeking in Context: Proceedings of an International Conference on Research in Information Needs, Seeking and Use in Different Contexts* (Tampere, Finland, Aug. 14-16, 1996) (pp. 236–256). London: Taylor Graham. 36, 38, 40, 50, 68, 69

Bartlett, J. C., Ishimura, Y., and Kloda, L. A. (2011). Why choose this one? Factors in scientists' selection of bioinformatics tools. *Information Research*, 16(1), paper 463. Retrieved from http://InformationR.net/ir/16-1/paper463.html. 36, 39, 40, 46, 47, 55, 58, 63, 66, 69, 70, 71

Bates, M. J. (2002). Toward an integrated model of information seeking and searching. *The New Review of Information Behaviour Research*, 3, 1–15. 3

Bauer, C. and Dey, A. K. (2016). Considering context in the design of intelligent systems: Current practices and suggestions for improvement. *Journal of Systems and Software*, 112, 26-47. DOI: 10.1016/j.jss.2015.10.041. 73

Bauer, J. S., Newman, M. W., and Kientz, J. A. (2014). What designers talk about when they talk about context. *Human–Computer Interaction*, 29(5–6), 420–450. DOI: 10.1080/07370024.2014.896709. 73

Beaulieu, M. (2006). Interaction in context in information research: Shifting the paradigm. In I. Ruthven, P. Borlund, P. Ingwersen, N. J. Belkin, A. Tombros, and P. Vakkari (Eds.), *Proceedings of the 1st International Conference on Information interaction in Context* (Copenhagen, Denmark, Oct. 18-20, 2006) (pp. 1–2). New York: ACM. DOI: 10.1145/1164820.1164822. 2

Belkin, N. J. (1984). Cognitive models and information transfer. *Social Science Information Studies*, 4(2–3), 111–129. DOI: 10.1016/0143-6236(84)90070-X. 3

Belkin, N. J. (1990). The cognitive viewpoint in information science. *Journal of Information Science*, 16, 11–15. DOI: 10.1177/016555159001600104. 5

Berryman, J. M. (2006). What defines 'enough' information? How policy workers make judgements and decisions during information seeking: preliminary results from an exploratory study. *Information Research*, 11(4), paper 266. Retrieved from http://InformationR.net/ir/11-4/paper266.html. 36, 38, 40, 48, 49, 50, 55, 71

Berryman, J. M. (2008). Influences on the judgement of enough information: an analysis using the information use environment as a framework. *Information Research*, 13(4), paper 356. Retrieved from http://InformationR.net/ir/13-4/paper356.html. 36, 38, 40, 48, 49, 50, 51, 52, 53, 55, 58, 61

Bhavani, S. K., Drabenstott, K., and Radev, D. (2001). Toward a unified framework of IR tasks and strategies. In T.B. Hahn (Ed.), *Proceedings of the Annual Meeting - American Society for Information Science*, 38 (pp. 340–354). Medford, NJ: Information Today. 54, 57

Borgman, C. L. (1989). All users of information retrieval systems are not created equal: an exploration into individual differences. *Information Processing and Management*, 25(3), 237–251. DOI: 10.1016/0306-4573(89)90042-3. 65, 66, 67

Borlund, P. (2003). The IIR evaluation model: a framework for evaluation of interactive information retrieval systems. *Information Research*, 8(3), paper no. 152. Retrieved from http://informationr.net/ir/8-3/paper152.html. 54

Borlund, P., Dreier, S., and Byström, K. (2012). What does time spent on searching indicate? In *Proceedings of the 4th Information Interaction in Context Symposium* (pp. 184–193). ACM. DOI: 10.1145/2362724.2362756. 37, 39, 40, 65, 67, 71

Brennan, K., Kelly, D., and Arguello, J. (2014). The effect of cognitive abilities on information search for tasks of varying levels of complexity. In *Proceedings of the 5th Information Interaction in Context Symposium* (pp. 165–174). ACM. DOI: 10.1145/2637002.2637022. 37, 38, 40, 44, 45, 63, 66

Brewer, M. (2000). Research Design and Issues of Validity. In Reis, H. and Judd, C. (eds.). *Handbook of Research Methods in Social and Personality Psychology*. New York: Cambridge University Press. 37

Brézillon, P. (1999). Context in problem solving: a survey. *Knowledge Engineering Review*. 14(1), 47–80. DOI: 10.1017/S0269888999141018. 13

Bronstein, J. (2010). Selecting and using information sources: source preferences and information pathways of Israeli library and information science students. *Information Research*, 15(4), paper 447. Retrieved from http://InformationR.net/ir/15-4/paper447.html. 36, 39, 40

Brown, E. (2010). Introduction to location-based mobile learning. In E. Brown (Ed.). *Education in the Wild: Contextual and Location-Based Mobile Learning in Action*. Learning Sciences Research Institute, University of Nottingham. 9, 46, 47, 58, 63, 66, 68, 69

Bruce, H., Fidel, R., Pejtersen, A. M., Dumais, S., Grudin, J., and Poltrock, S. (2003). A comparison of the collaborative information retrieval behaviour of two design teams. *The New Review of Information Behaviour Research*, 4(1), 139–153. DOI: 10.1080/14716310310001631499. 36, 40, 48, 49, 50, 52, 53, 55, 58

Byström, K. and Järvelin, K. (1995). Task complexity affects information seeking and use. *Information Processing and Management*, 31(2), 191–213. DOI: 10.1016/0306-4573(95)80035-R. 6, 24 , 34, 56, 58

Byström, K. (1997). Municipal administrators at work—information needs and seeking [IN&S] in relation to task complexity: a case-study amongst municipal officials. In P. Vakkari, R. Savolainen, and B. Dervin (Eds.). *Proceedings of an International Conference on Information*

Seeking in Context (pp. 125–146). London: Taylor Graham Publishing. 9, 36, 39, 40, 46, 47, 54, 57, 58

Byström, K. (2002). Information and information sources in tasks of varying complexity. *Journal of the American Society for Information Science and Technology*, 53, 581–591. DOI: 10.1002/asi.10064. 56

Byström, K., and Hansen, P. (2005). Conceptual framework for tasks in information studies. *Journal of the American Society for Information Science and Technology*, 56(10), 1050–1061. DOI: 10.1002/asi.20197. 5, 32, 53, 54, 55, 57

Callon, M. and Law, J. (1989). On the construction of sociotechnical networks: content and context revisited. *Knowledge and Society*. 8, 57–83. 79, 80

Campion, M. A., Medsker, G. J., and Higgs, C. A. (1993). Relations between work group characteristics and effectiveness. *Personnel Psychology*, 46, 823–850. DOI: 10.1111/j.1744-6570.1993.tb01571.x. 56, 58

Carston, R. (1999). *Herbert H. Clark, Using Language*. Cambridge: Cambridge University Press, 1996. 14

Case, D. O., Andrews, J. E., Johnson, J. D., and Allard, S. L. (2005). Avoiding versus seeking: the relationship of information seeking to avoidance, blunting, coping, dissonance, and related concepts. *Journal of the Medical Library Association*, 93(3), 353–362. 5

Case, D. O. and Given, L. M. (2016). *Looking for Information: A Survey of Research on Information Seeking, Needs, and Behavior* (Fourth Edition). Bingley, UK: Emerald Group Publishing. DOI: 10.1108/S2055-53772016. 3, 5, 25, 37, 41, 58, 59, 64, 66, 114, 129, 133

Case, D. O. (2010). A model of the information seeking and decision making of online coin buyers. *Information Research*, 15(4), paper 448. Retrieved from http://InformationR.net/ir/15-4/paper448.html. 10, 36, 39, 40, 50, 64, 66

Cavanagh, M. F. (2013). Interpreting reference work with contemporary practice theory. *Journal of Documentation*, 69(2), 214–242. DOI: 10.1108/00220411311300057. 48

Chatman, E. A. (1991). Life in a small world: Applicability of gratification theory to information-seeking behavior. *Journal of the American Society for Information Science*, 42, 438–449. DOI: 10.1002/(SICI)1097-4571(199107)42:6<438::AID-ASI6>3.0.CO;2-B. 25, 51

Chatman, E. A. (1992). *The Information World of Retired Women*. Westport, CT: Greenwood Press. 25

Chatman, E. A. (1996). The impoverished life-world of outsiders. *Journal of the American Society for Information Science*, 47, 193–206. 5, 13, 25, 51, 115

Chatman, E.A. (2000). Framing social life in theory and research. *New Review of Information Behavior Research*, 1, 3–17. 95

Chen, G. and Kotz, D. (2000). A survey of context-aware mobile computing research. *Dartmouth Computer Science Technical Report TR2000-381*. 19, 134

Chen, Y. and Jones, G. J. (2014). Are episodic context features helpful for refinding tasks?: Lessons learnt from a case study with lifelogs. In *Proceedings of the 5th Information Interaction in Context Symposium* (pp. 76–85). ACM. DOI: 10.1145/2637002.2637013. 74

Choo, C. and Auster, E. (1993). Environmental scanning: acquisition and use of information by managers. In M. Williams (Ed.), *Annual Review of Information Science and Technology* (pp.279–314). Medford, NJ: Learned Information. 10

Christensen, E. W. and Bailey, J. R. (1997). A source accessibility effect on media selection. *Management Communication Quarterly*, 10(3), 373–388. DOI: 10.1177/0893318997010003005. 67

Churchman, C. W. (1979). *The Systems Approach*. New York: Dell. 13

Clark, H. H. (1996). *Using Language*. Cambridge, UK: Cambridge University Press. DOI: 10.1017/CBO9780511620539. 14

Cole, C. (2012). Information need: a theory connecting information search to knowledge formation. *American Society for Information Science and Technology*. Medford, NJ: Information Today, Inc. 58, 59, 61

Cole, C. and Kuhlthau, C. (2000). Information and information seeking of novice versus expert lawyers: how experts add value. *The New Review of Information Behaviour Research*, 1(January), 103–115. 10

Cole, C., Behesthi, J., Large, A., Lamoureux, I., Abuhimed, D., and AlGhamdi, M. (2013). Seeking information for a middle school history project: The concept of implicit knowledge in the students' transition from Kuhlthau's Stage 3 to Stage 4. *Journal of the Association for Information Science and Technology*, 64(3), 558–573. 10

CollegeNet (2015). Texting someone in the same house. Are we doomed? CollegeNet. Retrieved from https://www.collegenet.com/elect/app/app?service=external/Forum&sp=75726#507863. 1

Collins-Thompson, K., Rieh, S. Y., Haynes, C. C., and Syed, R. (2016). Assessing learning outcomes in web search: A comparison of tasks and query strategies. In *Proceedings of the 2016 ACM Conference on Human Information Interaction and Retrieval* (pp. 163–172). ACM. DOI: 10.1145/2854946.2854972. 36, 38, 40, 50

Cook, J. (2010). Mobile learner generated contexts. Research on the internalization of the world of cultural products. In B. Bachmair (Ed.) *Medienbildung in Neuen Kulturräumen: Die Deutschsprachige und Britische Diskussion*, 113–126. Wiesbaden: VS Verlag für Sozialwissenschaften. DOI: 10.1007/978-3-531-92133-4_8. 16, 78

Cook, S. D. N. and Brown, J. S. (1999). Bridging epistemologies: the generative dance between organizational knowledge and organizational knowing. *Organization Science*, 10(4), 381–400. DOI: 10.1287/orsc.10.4.381. 4

Cool, C. (2001). The concept of situation in information science. *Annual Review of Information Science and Technology*, 35, 5–42. 2, 11, 75

Courtright, C. (2007). Context in information behavior research. *Annual Review of Information Science and Technology*, 41, 273–306. DOI: 10.1002/aris.2007.1440410113. 7, 8, 11, 41, 51, 53, 64, 66, 75, 78, 81, 84, 88, 90, 134

Cox, A. M. (2012). An exploration of the practice approach and its place in information science. *Journal of Information Science*, 38(2), 176–188. DOI: 10.1177/0165551511435881. 48

Crescenzi, A., Kelly, D., and Azzopardi, L. (2016). Impacts of time constraints and system delays on user experience. In *Proceedings of the 2016 ACM Conference on Human Information Interaction and Retrieval* (pp. 141–150). ACM. DOI: 10.1145/2854946.2854976. 36, 38, 48, 49, 50, 56, 58, 63, 66, 72, 112

Culnan, M. J. (1985). The dimensions of perceived accessibility to information: Implications for the delivery of information systems and services. *Journal of the American Society for Information Science*, 36, 302–308. DOI: 10.1002/asi.4630360504. 56, 58

Dahlstrom, D. O. (2013). *The Heidegger Dictionary*. London: A and C Black. 11, 78

Daoud, M., Tamine-Lechani, L., and Boughanem, M. (2008). Learning user interests for a session-based personalized search. In *Proceedings of the Second International Symposium on Information Interaction in Context* (pp. 57–64). ACM. DOI: 10.1145/1414694.1414708. 74

Davies, E. and McKenzie, P. J. (2004). Preparing for opening night: Temporal boundary objects in textually-mediated professional practice. *Information Research*, 10(1). Retrieved from http://informationr.net/ir/10-1/paper211.html. 9

Davis, F. D. (1989). Perceived usefulness, perceived ease of use, and user acceptance of information technology. *MIS Quarterly*, 13(3), 319–340. DOI: 10.2307/249008. 68, 69

Davis, J. L. and Jurgenson, N. (2014). Context collapse: Theorizing context collusions and collisions. *Information, Communication and Society*, 17(4), 476–485. DOI: 10.1080/1369118X.2014.888458. 17, 18, 27, 28

Dehghani, M., Azarbonyad, H., Kamps, J., and Marx, M. (2016). Generalized group profiling for content customization. In *Proceedings of the 2016 ACM Conference on Human Information Interaction and Retrieval* (pp. 245–248). ACM. DOI: 10.1145/2854946.2855003. 73

Dervin (1997). Given a context by any other name: Methodological tools for taming the unruly beast. In P. Vakkari, R. Savolainen, and B. Dervin (Eds.), *Information Seeking in Context: Proceedings of an International Conference on Research in Information Needs, Seeking and Use in Different Contexts* (Tampere, Finland, Aug. 14–16, 1996) (pp. 13–38). London: Taylor Graham. xix, 2, 7, 11, 75, 79, 81, 84, 90, 98, 119

Dervin, B. (1992). From the mind's eye of the user: the sense-making qualitative-quantitative methodology. In J. D. Glazier and R. R. Powell (Eds.), *Qualitative Research in Information Management* (pp.61–84). Englewood, CO: Libraries Unlimited. 5

Dervin, B. [ewuvideo] (Feb 2011). Connecting with Specific Publics: Treating Communication Communicatively. Eastern Spotlight: Brenda Dervin [Video File] Lecture at Les Schwab Room, the Spokane Arena, Eastern Washington University. Retrieved from http://youtu.be/foyH6eoIseQ. 123

Dervin, B. and Foreman-Wernet, L. (2012). Sense-making methodology as an approach to understanding and designing for campaign audiences. In R. E. Rice and C. K. Atkin (Eds.), *Public Communication Campaigns* (4th ed.) (pp.147–162). Los Angeles: Sage. 5, 28, 29, 34, 71

Dey, A. (2001). Understanding and Using Context. *Personal and Ubiquitous Computing*, 5(1), 4–7. DOI: 10.1007/s007790170019. 78, 134

Dey, A., Abowd, G., and Salber, D. (2001). A conceptual framework and a toolkit for supporting the rapid prototyping of context-aware applications. *Human-Computer Interaction*, 16(2–4), 97–166. DOI: 10.1207/S15327051HCI16234_02. 72

Dey, A. K. and Abowd, G. D. (1999). Toward a Better Understanding of Context and Context-Awareness. GVU Technical Report GIT-GVU-99-22, College of Computing, Georgia Institute of Technology. 6

Dixon, P. and Banwell, L. (1999). School governors and effective decision making. In T.D. Wilson and D.K. Allen (Eds.), *Exploring the Contexts of Information Behaviour* (pp. 384–392). London, UK: Taylor Graham Publishing. 36, 39, 40, 48, 49, 50, 52, 53, 64, 66

Dourish, P. (2004). What we talk about when we talk about context. *Personal and Ubiquitous Computing*, 8, 19–30. DOI: 10.1007/s00779-003-0253-8. 7, 8, 9, 11, 14, 16, 27, 39, 53 , 72, 73, 77, 78, 79, 80, 81, 84, 88, 90, 94, 119, 125, 134

Dourish, P. (2001). *Where the Action Is: The Foundations of Embodied Interaction*. Cambridge, MA: MIT Press. 52 , 72

Du, J. T., Liu, Y. H., Zhu, Q. H., and Chen, Y. J. (2013). Modelling marketing professionals' information behaviour in the workplace: toward a holistic understanding. *Information Research*, 18(1), paper 560. Retrieved from http://InformationR.net/ir/18-1/paper560.html. 36, 40, 46, 47, 68, 69, 70, 71

Duranti, A. and Goodwin, C. (Eds.) (1992). *Rethinking Context: Language as an Interactive Phenomenon* (Vol. 11). Cambridge University Press. 134

Edwards, A. and Kelly, D. (2016). How does interest in a work task impact search behavior and engagement? In *Proceedings of the 2016 ACM Conference on Human Information Interaction and Retrieval* (pp. 249–252). ACM. DOI: 10.1145/2854946.2855000. 36, 38, 44, 45, 56, 58

Edwards, C., Fox, R., Gillard, S., Gourlay, S., Guven, P., Jackson, C., Chambers, M., and Drennan, V. (2013). *Explaining Health Managers' Information Seeking Behaviour and Use*. Final report. London: National Institute for Health Research, Service Delivery and Organisation programme. 10

Eickhoff, C., Dekker, P., and De Vries, A. P. (2012). Supporting children's web search in school environments. In *Proceedings of the 4th Information Interaction in Context Symposium* (pp. 129–137). ACM. DOI: 10.1145/2362724.2362748. 37, 38, 40, 44, 45, 63, 65, 66, 67

Ellis, D. (1989). A behavioral approach to information retrieval design. *Journal of Documentation*, 45, 171–212. DOI: 10.1108/eb026843. 5

Ellis, D. (2011). The emergence of conceptual modelling in information behaviour research. In A. Spink and J. Heinström (Eds.), *New Directions in Information Behaviour* (pp. 17–35). Bingley, UK: Emerald. DOI: 10.1108/S1876-0562(2011)002011a005. 5

Enwald, H., Hirvonen, N., Korpelainen, R. and Huotari, M-L. (2015). Young men's perceptions of fear appeal versus neutral health messages: associations with everyday health information literacy, education, and health. In *Proceedings of ISIC, the Information Behaviour Conference*, Leeds, Sept. 2–5, 2014: Part 2 (paper isic22). Retrieved from http://InformationR. net/ir/20-1/isic2/isic22.html. 37, 40, 42, 43, 64, 66

Erdelez, S. (1997). Information encountering a conceptual framework for accidental information discovery. In Vakkari, P., Savolainen, R., and Dervin, B. (eds.), *Information Seeking in Context. Proceedings of an International Conference on Research in Information Needs, Seeking and Use in Different Contexts*, (pp. 412–421) London: Taylor Graham, 412–421. 4

Erdelez, S., Beheshti, J., Heinström, J., Toms, E., Makri, S., Agarwal, N. K., and Björneborn, L. (2016). *Research Perspectives on Serendipity and Information Encountering. Annual Meeting of the Association for Information Science and Technology (ASIS&T 2016)* (Copenhagen, Denmark, Oct. 14–18, 2016). Retrieved from https://www.asist.org/files/meetings/am16/proceedings/submissions/panels/11panel.pdf. 4

Farganis, J. (2011). *Readings in Social Theory: The Classic Tradition to Post-Modernism* (6th ed.). New York: McGraw-Hill. 117

Fatemi, F. (2015). The future of the web is all about context. *Tech Crunch - Crunch Network*, Aug. 18, 2015. Retrieved from https://techcrunch.com/2015/08/18/the-future-of-the-web-is-all-about-context/. 2

Feng, L., Apers, P. M., and Jonker, W. (2004). Toward context-aware data management for ambient intelligence. In *International Conference on Database and Expert Systems Applications* (pp. 422–431). Berlin Heidelberg: Springer. DOI: 10.1007/978-3-540-30075-5_41. 51, 62

Fidel, R. and Pejtersen, A. M. (2004). From information behaviour research to the design of information systems: The cognitive work analysis framework. *Information Research*, 10(1), paper 210. Retrieved from http://InformationR.net/ir/10-1/paper210.html. 13

Fidel, R. (2012). *Human Information Interaction: An Ecological Approach to Information Behavior.* Cambridge, MA: MIT Press. DOI: 10.7551/mitpress/9780262017008.001.0001. 2, 6, 19, 75

Fisher, K., Naumer, C., Durrance, J., Stromski, L. and Christiansen, T. (2005). Something old, something new: preliminary findings from an exploratory study about people's information habits and information grounds. *Information Research*, 10(2), paper 223. Retrieved from http://InformationR.net/ir/10-2/paper223.html. 15

Fisher, K. E., Durrance, J. C., and Hinton, M. B. (2004). Information grounds and the use of need-based services by immigrants in Queens, NY: a context-based, outcome evaluation approach. *Journal of the American Society for Information Science and Technology*, 55(8), 754–766. DOI: 10.1002/asi.20019. 15, 16

Fisher, K. E., Landry, C. F., and Naumer, C. (2006). Social spaces, casual interactions, meaningful exchanges: 'information ground' characteristics based on the college student experience. *Information Research*, 12(2) paper 291. Retrieved from http://InformationR.net/ir/12-1/paper291.html. 15

Ford, N. and Chen, S. Y. (2000). Individual differences, hypermedia navigation, and learning: an empirical study. *Journal of Educational Multimedia and Hypermedia*, 9(4), 282–311. 63, 66

Ford, N. (2015). *Introduction to Information Behaviour*. London: Facet Publishing. 3

Foreman-Wernet, L. (2003). Rethinking Communication: Introducing the Sense-Making Methodology. In B. Dervin and L. Foreman-Wernet with E. Lauterbach (Eds.). *Sense-Making Methodology Reader: Selected Writings of Brenda Dervin* (Chapter 1, pp. 3–16). Cresskill, NJ: Hampton Press. 3, 28, 62, 87

Fourie, I. and Julien H. (2014). Ending the dance: a research agenda for affect and emotion in studies of information behaviour; In *Proceedings of ISIC, the Information Behaviour Conference*, Leeds, 2–5 September, 2014: Part 1 (paper isic09). Retrieved from http://InformationR.net/ir/19-4/isic/isic09.html. 65

Fransson, J. (2012). Intention and task context connected with session in a cultural heritage collection. In *Proceedings of the 4th Information Interaction in Context Symposium* (pp. 138–144). ACM. DOI: 10.1145/2362724.2362750. 37, 40, 42, 43, 55, 58, 65, 66

Galeana-Zapién, H., Torres-Huitzil, C., and Rubio-Loyola, J. (2014). Mobile phone middleware architecture for energy and context awareness in location-based services. *Sensors*. 14(12), 23673–23696. DOI: 10.3390/s141223673. 74

Gerstenberger, P. G. and Allen, T. J. (1968). Criteria used by research and development engineers in selection of an information source. *Journal of Applied Psychology*, 52(4), 272–279. DOI: 10.1037/h0026041. 59, 61

Golovchinsky, G., Diriye, A., and Dunnigan, T. (2012). The future is in the past: designing for exploratory search. In *Proceedings of the 4th Information Interaction in Context Symposium* (pp. 52–61). ACM. DOI: 10.1145/2362724.2362738. 73

Gorman, P. (1999). Information seeking of primary care physicians: Conceptual models and empirical studies. *Proceedings of the Second International Conference on Research in Information Needs, Seeking and Use in Different Contexts*, 226–240. 10

Gossen, T., Höbel, J., and Nürnberger, A. (2014). Usability and perception of young users and adults on targeted web search engines. In *Proceedings of the 5th Information Interaction in Context Symposium* (pp. 18–27). ACM. DOI: 10.1145/2637002.2637007. 37, 38, 40, 44, 45, 63, 66

Grad, R., Pluye, P., Granikov, V., Johnson-Lafleur, J., Shulha, M., Sridhar, S. B., Moscovici, J. L., Bartlett, G., Vandal, A. C., Marlow, B., and Kloda, L. (2011). Physicians' assessment of the value of clinical information: Operationalization of a theoretical model. *Journal of the Association for Information Science and Technology*, 62(10), 1884–1891. 10

Gray, P. H. and Meister, D. B. (2004). Knowledge sourcing effectiveness. *Management Science*, 50(6), 821–834. DOI: 10.1287/mnsc.1030.0192. 56, 58, 64, 65, 66, 67

Guha, R. V. and Lenat, D. B. (1994). Enabling agents to work together. *Communications of the ACM*. 37(7), 126–42. DOI: 10.1145/176789.176804. 17

Gyllstrom, K. and Moens, M. F. (2012). Surfin' Wikipedia: an analysis of the Wikipedia (non-random) surfer's behavior from aggregate access data. In *Proceedings of the 4th Information Interaction in Context Symposium* (pp. 155–163). ACM. DOI: 10.1145/2362724.2362752. 48, 49, 50

Gyllstrom, K., Soules, C., and Veitch, A. (2008). Activity put in context: identifying implicit task context within the user's document interaction. In *Proceedings of the Second International Symposium on Information Interaction in Context* (pp. 51–56). ACM. DOI: 10.1145/1414694.1414707. 73

Heineken International [Heineken]. (2017). Heineken | Worlds Apart | #OpenYourWorld [Video File]. Retrieved from http://youtu.be/8wYXw4K0A3g. 113

Heisenberg, W. (1958). Physics and philosophy: The revolution in modern science. In R.N. Anshen (Series Ed.) *World Perspectives No. 15*. London, UK: John Dickens and Co. Ltd. 84

Hinton, A. (2014). *Understanding Context: Environment, Language, and Information Architecture.* Sebastopol, CA: O'Reilly Media. 134

Hinze, A. and Buchanan, G. (2005). Context-awareness in mobile tourist information systems: challenges for user interaction. In *International Workshop on Context in Mobile HCI at the Seventh International Conference on Human Computer Interaction with Mobile Devices and Services*, Salzburg. New York: ACM Press, pp. 257–266. 72

Hofstede, G. (1980). *Culture's Consequences.* Beverly Hills, CA: Sage. 100, 122

Holton, M. A. and Curry, C. M. (1914). *Holton-Curry Readers: The Fourth Reader.* Chicago, IL: Rand McNally and Company. 82

Hughes-Morgan, K., and Wilson, M. L. (2012). Information vs interaction: examining different interaction models over consistent metadata. In *Proceedings of the 4th Information Interaction in Context Symposium* (pp. 72–81). ACM. DOI: 10.1145/2362724.2362740. 36, 37, 40, 44, 45, 69

Hultgren, F. and Limberg, L. (2003). A study of research on children's information behaviour in a school context. *The New Review of Information Behaviour Research*, 4(1), 1–15. DOI: 10.1080/14716310310001631408. 42

Huurdeman, H. C., Wilson, M. L., and Kamps, J. (2016). Active and passive utility of search interface features in different information seeking task stages. In *Proceedings of the 2016 ACM Conference on Human Information Interaction and Retrieval* (pp. 3–12). ACM. DOI: 10.1145/2854946.2854957. 36, 38, 40, 44, 45, 55, 58

Ingwersen, P. and Järvelin, K. (2005). *The Turn: Integration of Information Seeking and Retrieval in Context.* Dordrecht, The Netherlands: Springer. 2, 5, 13, 19, 22, 51, 68, 69, 71, 79, 98, 121

Ingwersen, P. (1992). *Information Retrieval Interaction*. London: Taylor Graham. 5

Ingwersen, P. (2005). Selected variables for IR interaction in context: Introduction to IRiX SIGIR 2005 Workshop. In *Proceedings of the ACM SIGIR 2005 Workshop on Information Retrieval in Context (IRiX)* (Salvador, Brazil, Aug. 19) (pp. 6–9), New York: ACM. 98

Ingwersen, P., Ruthven, I., and Belkin, N. (2007). First international symposium on information interaction in context. Conference report. *ACM SIGIR Forum*, 41(1), 117–119. 75

Inwood, M. J. (1999). *A Heidegger Dictionary*. Hoboken, NJ: Wiley. DOI: 10.1111/b.9780631190 950.1999.x. 11

Ishimura, Y. and Bartlett. J. C. (2013). Uncovering the research process of international students in North America: are they different from domestic students? *Information Research*, 18(1), paper 564. Retrieved from http://InformationR.net/ir/18-1/paper564.html. 36, 40, 48, 49, 50, 52, 53, 55, 58, 64, 66, 67

Janes, J. and Silverstein, J. (2003). Question negotiation and the technological environment. *D-Lib Magazine*, 9(2). DOI: 10.1045/february2003-janes. 9

Jansen, B. J. and Rieh, S. Y. (2010). The seventeen theoretical constructs of information searching and information retrieval. *Journal of the American Society for Information Science and Technology*, 61(8), 1517–1534. DOI: 10.1002/asi.21358. 6

Jansen, B. J., Jung, S. -G., Salminen, J., An, J., and Kwak, H. (2017, forthcoming). Viewed by Too Many or Viewed Too Little: Using Information Dissemination for Audience Segmentation. In *Proceedings of the 80th Annual Meeting of the Association for Information Science and Technology* (Washington, D.C., Oct 27-Nov 1). 90

Jarrahi, M. H. and Thomson, L. (2017). The interplay between information practices and information context: The case of mobile knowledge workers. *Journal of the Association for Information Science and Technology*, 68(5), 1073–1089. DOI: 10.1002/asi.23773. 48

Järvelin, K. and Ingwersen, P. (2004). Information seeking research needs extension toward tasks and technology. *Information Research*, 10(1), paper 212. Retrieved from http://InformationR.net/ir/10-1/paper212.html. 2, 5

Järvelin, K. (2007). An analysis of two approaches in information retrieval: from frameworks to study designs. *Journal of the American Society for Information Science and Technology*, 58(7), 971–986. DOI: 10.1002/asi.20589. 5

Johnson, J. D. (1997). *Cancer-related Information Seeking*. Cresskill, NJ: Hampton Press. 5

Johnson, J. D. E., Case, D. O., Andrews, J., Allard, S. L., and Johnson, N. E. (2006). Fields and pathways Contrasting or complementary views of information seeking. *Information Processing and Management*, 42(2), 569–582. DOI: 10.1016/j.ipm.2004.12.001. 12, 13, 78

Johnson, J. D. (2003). On contexts of information seeking. *Information Processing and Management*, 39, 735–760. DOI: 10.1016/S0306-4573(02)00030-4. 7, 75

Johnson, J. D. and Case, D. O. (2012). *Health Information Seeking*. New York: Peter Lang Inc. 114

Joho, H., Hannah, D., and Jose, J. M. (2008). Comparing collaborative and independent search in a recall-oriented task. In *Proceedings of the Second International Symposium on Information Interaction in Context* (pp. 89–96). ACM. DOI: 10.1145/1414694.1414715. 36, 38, 40

Jumisko-Pyykkö, S. and Vainio, T. (2010). Framing the Context of Use for Mobile HCI. *International Journal of Mobile Human Computer Interaction*. 2(4), 1–28. DOI: 10.4018/jmhci.2010100101. 32, 33, 34, 51, 67, 72, 73, 80, 127

Kahneman, D. (2011). *Thinking Fast and Slow*. New York: Farrar, Straus and Giroux. 81

Kari, J. and Savolainen, R. (2003). Toward a contextual model of information seeking on the Web. *New Review of Information Behavior Research*, 4(1), 155–175. DOI: 10.1080/14716310310001631507. 5, 13, 14, 121

Karunakaran, A., Reddy, M. C., and Spence, P. R. (2013). Toward a model of collaborative information behavior in organizations. *Journal of the American Society for Information Science and Technology*, 64(12), 2437–2451. DOI: 10.1002/asi.22943. 5, 31, 32, 34, 53

Keith, W. M. (1994). Review of: Communication at a distance: The influence of print on socio-cultural evolution and change. *Quarterly Journal of Speech*, 80, 229–232. 2

Kekäläinen, J., Arvola, P., and Kumpulainen, S. (2014). Browsing patterns in retrieved documents. In *Proceedings of the 5th Information Interaction in Context Symposium* (pp. 299–302). ACM. DOI: 10.1145/2637002.2637047. 42

Kim, K. -S. and Allen, B. (2002). Cognitive and task influences on Web searching behavior. *Journal of the American Society for Information Science and Technology*, 53(2), 109–119. DOI: 10.1002/asi.10014. 53

Kim, K. -S. and Sin, S. -C. J. (2015). Use of social media in different contexts of information seeking: effects of sex and problem-solving style. In *Proceedings of ISIC, the Information Behaviour Conference* (Leeds, Sept. 2-5, 2014). Part 2 (paper isic24). Retrieved from http://InformationR.net/ir/20-1/isic2/isic24.html. 36, 37, 40, 46, 47, 60, 61, 63, 66

Kim, K. -S. (2000). Users, tasks and the Web: Their impact on the information-seeking behavior. *Proceedings of the 21st National Online Meeting* (New York, May 16–18, 2000), 189–198. 54, 57

Kiseleva, J., Williams, K., Jiang, J., Hassan Awadallah, A., Crook, A. C., Zitouni, I., and Anastasakos, T. (2016). Understanding user satisfaction with intelligent assistants. In *Proceedings of the 2016 ACM Conference on Human Information Interaction and Retrieval* (pp. 121–130). ACM. DOI: 10.1145/2854946.2854961. 38, 40, 54, 57, 58, 69, 112

Krikelas, J. (1983). Information-seeking behavior: patterns and concepts. *Drexel Library Quarterly*, 19, 5–20. 5, 101

Kuhlthau, C. (1993). A principle of uncertainty for information seeking. *Journal of Documentation*, 49, 339–355. DOI: 10.1108/eb026918. 22, 23

Kuhlthau, C. C. (1991). Inside the search process: information seeking from the user's perspective. *Journal of the American Society for Information Science*, 42(5), 361–371. DOI: 10.1002/(SICI)1097-4571(199106)42:5<361::AID-ASI6>3.0.CO;2-#. 5, 38, 45, 55, 58

Kuutti, K. (1999). Activity theory, transformation of work, and information systems design. In Y. Engeström, R. Miettinen, and R.-L. Punamäki-Gitai (Eds.), *Perspectives on Activity Theory. Learning in Doing: Social, Cognitive and Computational Perspectives* (pp. 360–376). Cambridge, UK: Cambridge University Press. DOI: 10.1017/CBO9780511812774.024. 7

Kwasitsu, L. (2003). Information-seeking behavior of design, process, and manufacturing engineers. *Library and Information Science Research*, 25, 459–476. DOI: 10.1016/S0740-8188(03)00054-9. 64, 66

Lakoff, G. and Johnson, M. (1999). *Philosophy in the Flesh: The Embodied Mind and its Challenge to Western Thought*. New York: Basic Books. 52

Lakshminarayanan, B. (2010). Toward developing an integrated model of information behaviour (Doctoral dissertation). Retrieved from QUT ePrints. (33252). 51

Lamb, R., King, J. L., and Kling, R. (2003). Informational environments: Organizational contexts of online information use. *Journal of the American Society for Information Science and Technology*, 54, 97–114. DOI: 10.1002/asi.10182. 9, 51, 119

Lamsfus, C., Wang, D., Alzua-Sorzabal, A., and Xiang, Z. (2015). Going mobile: Defining context for on-the-go travelers. *Journal of Travel Research*, 54(6), 691–701. DOI: 10.1177/0047287514538839. 128

Latham, K. F. (2014). Experiencing documents. *Journal of Documentation*, 70(4), 544–561. DOI: 10.1108/JD-01-2013-0013. 4

Lawrence, P. and Lorsch, J. (1967). *Organizations and Environment*. Cambridge, MA: Harvard University Press. 56, 58

Lea, M., O'Shea, T., and Fung, P. (1995). Constructing the networked organization: content and context in the development of electronic communications. *Organization Science*. 6(4), 462–478. DOI: 10.1287/orsc.6.4.462. 79, 80

Leckie, G. J. and Pettigrew, K. E. (1997). A general model of the information seeking of professionals: role theory through the back door?. In P. Vakkari, R. Savolainen and B. Dervin (eds.), *Information Seeking in Context: Proceedings of an International Conference on Research in Information Needs, Seeking and Use in Different Contexts* (Tampere, Finland, Aug. 14-16, 1996) (pp. 99–110). London: Taylor Graham. 10

Leckie, G. J., Pettigrew, K. E., and Sylvain, C. (1996). Modeling the information seeking of professionals: a general model derived from research on engineers, health care professionals and lawyers. *Library Quarterly*, 66, 161–193. DOI: 10.1086/602864. 5, 23, 24, 34

Lee, C. A. (2011). A framework for contextual information in digital collections. *Journal of Documentation*, 67(1), 96–143. DOI: 10.1108/00220411111105470. 2, 7, 9, 11, 17, 19, 78, 79, 80, 126

Lee, S., Shah, A., and Yoon, W. C. (2014). Visual information search based on knowledge schema modeling. In *Proceedings of the 5th Information Interaction in Context Symposium* (pp. 219–222). ACM. DOI: 10.1145/2637002.2641199. 73

Lievrouw, L. A. (2001). New media and the pluralization of life-worlds' a role for information in social differentiation. *New Media & Society*, 3(1), 7–28. 13

Limbu, D. K., Connor, A., Pears, R., and MacDonell, S. (2006). Contextual relevance feedback in web information retrieval. In *Proceedings of the 1st International Conference on Information interaction in Context* (pp. 138–143). ACM. DOI: 10.1145/1164820.1164848. 73

Lindblom, J. and Ziemke, T. (2003). Social situatedness of natural and artificial intelligence: Vygotsky and beyond. *Adaptive Behavior*, 11(2), 79–96. DOI: 10.1177/10597123030112002. 7, 11

Line, M. B. (1974). Draft definitions: information and library needs, wants, demands and uses. *Aslib Proceedings*, 26(2), 87. DOI: 10.1108/eb050451. 58, 59, 61

Lingel, J. (2015). Information practices of urban newcomers: An analysis of habits and wandering. *Journal of the Association for Information Science and Technology*, 66(6), 1239–1251. DOI: 10.1002/asi.23255. 48

Lioma, C., Larsen, B., and Ingwersen, P. (2012). Preliminary experiments using subjective logic for the polyrepresentation of information needs. In *Proceedings of the 4th Information Interaction in Context Symposium* (pp. 174–183). ACM. DOI: 10.1145/2362724.2362755. 74

Litt, E. and Hargittai, E. (2016). The imagined audience on social network sites. *Social Media + Society*, 2(1), 1–12. DOI: 10.1177/2056305116633482. 17, 18, 27

Liu, C., Yang, F., Zhao, Y., Jiang, Q., and Zhang, L. (2014). What does time constraint mean to information searchers? In *Proceedings of the 5th Information Interaction in Context Symposium* (pp. 227–230). ACM. DOI: 10.1145/2637002.2637029. 36, 38, 40, 65, 67, 71

Liu, H., Mulholland, P., Song, D., Uren, V., and Rüger, S. (2010). Applying information foraging theory to understand user interaction with content-based image retrieval. In *Proceedings of the Third Symposium on Information Interaction in Context* (pp. 135–144). ACM. DOI: 10.1145/1840784.1840805. 36, 37, 40, 44, 45, 54, 57

Lloyd, A., Bonner, A., and Dawson-Rose, C. (2014). The health information practices of people living with chronic health conditions: Implications for health literacy. *Journal of Librarianship and Information Science*, 46(3), 207–216. DOI: 10.1177/0961000613486825. 48

Lueg, C. (2002). On problem solving and information seeking. *New Review of Information Behavior Research*, 3, 99–112. 7 , 75

MacFarlane, A., Albrair, A., Marshall, C. R., and Buchanan, G. (2012). Phonological working memory impacts on information searching: An investigation of dyslexia. In *Proceedings of the 4th Information Interaction in Context Symposium* (pp. 27–34). ACM. DOI: 10.1145/2362724.2362734. 37, 40, 43, 45, 63

Mackenzie, M. L. (2005). Managers look to the social network to seek information. *Information Research*, 10(2), paper 216. Retrieved from http://InformationR.net/ir/10-2/paper216.html. 36, 39, 40, 46, 47, 69, 70, 71

MacKinnon, D. P. (2011). Integrating Mediators and Moderators in Research Design. *Research on Social Work Practice*, 21(6), 675–681. DOI: 10.1177/1049731511414148. 25, 42, 109

Makri, S. and Blandford, A. (2012). Coming across information serendipitously - Part I A process model. *Journal of Documentation*, 68(5), 684–705. DOI: 10.1108/00220411211256030. 4

Makri, S., Blandford, A., Woods, M., Sharples, S., and Maxwell, D. (2014). "Making my own luck" Serendipity strategies and how to support them in digital information environments. *Journal of the Association for Information Science and Technology*, 65(11), 2179–2194. DOI: 10.1002/asi.23200. 4

Marchionini, G. (1989). Information seeking strategies of novices using a full-text electronic encyclopedia. *Journal of the American Society for Information Science*, 40(1), 54–66. DOI: 10.1002/(SICI)1097-4571(198901)40:1<54::AID-ASI6>3.0.CO;2-R. 54, 57

Matthews, J. R., Lawrence, G. S., and Ferguson, D. K. (1983). *Using Online Catalogs: A Nation Wide Survey*. New York: Neal-Schumann. 54, 57

McCreadie, M. and Rice, R. E. (1999). Trends in analyzing access to information. Part I: cross-disciplinary conceptualizations of access. *Information Processing & Management*, 35(1), 45–76. 11

McKenzie, P. J. (2003). A model of information practices in accounts of everyday-life information seeking. *Journal of Documentation*, 59(1), 19–40. DOI: 10.1108/00220410310457993. 5, 29, 30, 34McKenzie, P. J. (2004). Positioning theory and the negotiation of information needs in a clinical midwifery setting. *Journal of the Association for Information Science and Technology*, 55, 684–694. 9

Mikkonen, A. and Vakkari, P. (2012). Readers' search strategies for accessing books in public libraries. In *Proceedings of the 4th Information Interaction in Context Symposium* (pp. 214–223). ACM. DOI: 10.1145/2362724.2362760. 37, 40, 42, 43, 63, 66

Miller, V. D. and Jablin, F. M. (1991). Information seeking during organizational entry: Influences, tactics, and a model of the process. *Academy of Management Review*, 16, 92–120. DOI: 10.5465/AMR.1991.4278997. 64, 66, 70

Mitchell, S. (1998). *Tao Te Ching by Lao-tzu: A New English Version*. New York: HarperPerennial. 115

Morrison, E. W. and Vancouver, J. B. (2000). Within-person analysis of information seeking: The effects of perceived costs and benefits. *Journal of Management*, 26, 119–137. DOI: 10.1177/014920630002600101. 65, 67

Morrison, E. W. (1993). Newcomer information seeking: Exploring types, modes, sources, and outcome. *Academy of Management Review*, 36, 557–589. DOI: 10.2307/256592. 59

Nahl, D. and Bilal, D. (Eds.). (2007). *Information and Emotion: The Emergent Affective Paradigm in Information Behavior Research and Theory*. Medford, NJ: Information Today. 5, 65, 67

NAIS (2017). *Sample Cultural Identifiers*. National Association of Independent Schools. Retrieved from https://www.nais.org/articles/pages/sample-cultural-identifiers.aspx. 62

Natarajan, N., Shin, D., and Dhillon, I. S. (2013). Which app will you use next?: collaborative filtering with interactional context. In *Proceedings of the 7th ACM Conference on Recommender Systems* (pp. 201–208). ACM. DOI: 10.1145/2507157.2507186. 16

Nissenbaum, H. (2010). *Privacy in Context: Technology, Policy, and the Integrity of Social Life*. Standford, CA: Standford University Press. 18

O'Reilly, C. A., III (1982). Variations in decision makers' use of information sources: The impact of quality and accessibility of information. *Academy of Management Journal*, 25(4), 756–771. DOI: 10.2307/256097. 56, 58, 59, 61

Olsson, M. (2016). Making sense of the past: The embodied information practices of field archaeologists. *Journal of Information Science*, 42(3), 410–419. DOI: 10.1177/0165551515621839. 48

Orlikowski, W. J. (2002). Knowing in practice: enacting a collective capability in distributed organizing. *Organization Science*, 13(3), 249–273. DOI: 10.1287/orsc.13.3.249.2776. 4

Paisley, W. J. (1968). Information Needs and Uses. In C.A. Caudra (ed.) *Annual Review of Information Science and Technology*, Vol. 3 (pp. 1–30), Chicago, IL: Encyclopaedia Britannica. 121

Pang, N. (2014). Crisis-based information seeking: Monitoring versus blunting in the information seeking behaviour of working students during the Southeast Asian Haze Crisis. In *Proceedings of ISIC, the Information Behaviour Conference*, (Leeds, Sept. 2–5, 2014). Part 1 (paper isic14). Retrieved from http://www.informationr.net/ir/19-4/isic/isic14.html. 36, 37, 40, 42, 43, 66

Pettigrew, K. E. (1999). Waiting for chiropody: contextual results from an ethnographic study of the information behaviour among attendees at community clinics. *Information Processing & Management*, 35(6), 801–817. 15

Pettigrew, K. E. (2000). Lay information provision in community settings: how community health nurses disseminate human services information to the elderly. *Library Quarterly: Information, Community, Policy*, 70(1), 47–85. DOI: 10.1086/603154. 9

Pettigrew, K. E., Fidel, R., and Bruce, H. (2001). Conceptual frameworks in information behavior. In E.W. Martha (Ed.), *Annual Review of Information Science and Technology* (pp. 35, 43-78). Medford, NJ: Information Today. 5, 70

Pfaffenberger, B. (1996). *Web Search Strategies*. New York: MIS Press. 54, 57

Pharo, N. and Nordlie, R. (2012). Examining the effect of task stage and topic knowledge on searcher interaction with a digital bookstore. In *Proceedings of the 4th Information Interaction in Context Symposium* (pp. 4–11). ACM. DOI: 10.1145/2362724.2362730. 36, 38, 40, 44, 45, 55, 58, 64, 66

Polanyi, M. (1967). *The Tacit Dimension*. London: Routledge and Kegan Paul. 60, 61

Qiu, L. (1993). Analytical searching vs. browsing in hypertext information retrieval systems. *Canadian Journal of Information and Library Science*, 18(4), 1–13. 54, 57

Renear, A. H. and Palmer, C. L. (2009). Strategic reading, ontologies, and the future of scientific publishing. *Science*, 325(5942), 828–832. DOI: 10.1126/science.1157784. 4

Rieh, S. Y. (2004). On the Web at home: Information seeking and Web searching in the home environment. *Journal of the American Society for Information Science and Technology*, 55, 743–753. DOI: 10.1002/asi.20018. 9, 51, 119

Ritzer, G. (2011). *Sociological Theory*. New York: McGraw-Hill. 117

Roberts, J. and Dietrich, M. (1999). Conceptualizing professionalism: Why economics needs sociology. *The American Journal of Economics and Sociology*, 58(4), 977–998. DOI: 10.1111/j.1536-7150.1999.tb03404.x. 60, 61

Robertson, S. E. (1981). The methodology of information retrieval experiment. In K. Spärck Jones (Ed.), *Information Retrieval Experiment* (pp. 9–31). London: Butterworths. 3

Ruthven, I. (2008). The context of the interface. In P. Borlund, J. W. Schneider, M. Lalmas, A. Tombros, J. Feather, D. Kelly, A. de Vries, and L. Azzopardi (Eds.), *Proceedings of the 2nd International Symposium on Information Interaction in Context* (London, Oct. 14-17, 2008) (pp. 3–5). New York: ACM. DOI: 10.1145/1414694.1414697. 2, 73

Ruthven, I., Borlund, P., Ingwersen, P., Belkin, N. J., Tombros, A., and Vakkari, P. (Eds.). (2006). *Proceedings of the 1st International Conference on Information interaction in Context* (Copenhagen, Denmark, Oct. 18–20, 2006). New York: ACM. DOI: 10.1145/1164820. 2

Saastamoinen, M., Kumpulainen, S., and Järvelin, K. (2012). Task complexity and information searching in administrative tasks revisited. In *Proceedings of the 4th Information Interaction in Context Symposium* (pp. 204–213). ACM. DOI: 10.1145/2362724.2362759. 36, 39, 40, 46, 47, 56, 58, 64, 66

Sacks, H. (1984). On doing 'being ordinary'. In Atkinson and Heritage (Eds.), *Structures of Social Action* (pp. 413–429). New York: Cambridge University Press. 14, 15, 39, 73

Salkind, N. J. (Ed.) (2010). *Encyclopedia of Research Design*. (Vol. 1-3). Thousand Oaks, CA: Sage Publications. DOI: 10.4135/9781412961288. 25, 109

Saracevic, T. and Kantor, P. (1988). A study of information seeking and retrieving II. Users, questions, and effectiveness. *Journal of the American Society for Information Science*, 39(3), 177–196. DOI: 10.1002/(SICI)1097-4571(198805)39:3<177::AID-ASI3>3.0.CO;2-F. 54, 57, 58

Saracevic, T. (1996). Modeling interaction in information retrieval (IR): a review and proposal. In S. Hardin (Ed.), *59th Annual Meeting of the American Society for Information Science* (pp. 3–9). Silver Spring, MD: American Society for Information Science. 5

Sarrafzadeh, B., Vtyurina, A., Lank, E., and Vechtomova, O. (2016). Knowledge graphs versus hierarchies: An analysis of user behaviours and perspectives in information seeking. In *Proceedings of the 2016 ACM Conference on Human Information Interaction and Retrieval* (pp. 91–100). ACM. DOI: 10.1145/2854946.2854958. 36, 38, 40, 44, 45, 54, 57, 64, 66, 69

Savolainen, R. (1995). Everyday life information seeking: Approaching information seeking in the context of "way of life". *Library and Information Science Research*, 17(3), 259–294. DOI: 10.1016/0740-8188(95)90048-9. 6, 25, 26, 34, 59, 61

Savolainen, R. (2007). Information behavior and information practice: Reviewing the "umbrella concepts" of information-seeking studies. *Library Quarterly*, 77(2), 109–132. DOI: 10.1086/517840. 5, 48

Savolainen, R. (2008). *Everyday Life Information Practices: A Social Phenomenological Perspective.* Lanham, MD: Scarecrow Press. 5, 47, 48

Savolainen, R. (2009). Epistemic work and knowing in practice as conceptualizations of information use. *Information Research*, 14(1), Paper 392. 4

Savolainen, R. (2012). Conceptualizing information need in context. Information Research, 17(4), paper 534. Retrieved from http://InformationR.net/ir/17-4/paper534.html. 3, 15, 59, 60, 81

Savolainen, R. (2014). Emotions as motivators for information seeking: a conceptual analysis. *Library and Information Science Research*, 36, 59–65. DOI: 10.1016/j.lisr.2013.10.004. 5

Savolainen, R. (2016). Approaching the affective barriers to information seeking: the viewpoint of appraisal theory. In *Proceedings of ISIC, the Information Behaviour Conference* (Zadar, Croatia, Sept. 20–23, 2016). Part 1. Information Research, 21(4), paper isic1603. Retrieved from http://InformationR.net/ir/21-4/isic/isic1603.html. 65

Schaller, R., Harvey, M., and Elsweiler, D. (2014). Relating user interaction to experience during festivals. In *Proceedings of the 5th Information Interaction in Context Symposium* (pp. 38–47). ACM. DOI: 10.1145/2637002.2637009. 37, 40, 44, 45, 59, 61

Schatzki, T. R., Knorr Cetina, K., and von Savigny, E. (2001). *The Practice Turn in Contemporary Theory.* London: Routledge. 48

Schmidt, A., Beigl, M., and Gellesen, H. -W. (1998). There is more to context than location. *International Workshop on Interactive Applications of Mobile Computing*, pp. 893–901. 19

Schütz, A. (1967). *Phenomenology of the Social World. Studies in Phenomenology and Existential Philosophy* (G. Walsh and F. Lehnert, Trans.). Evanston, IL: Northwestern University Press. 92, 117, 120, 130

Schütz, A., and Luckmann, T. (1973). *Structures of the Life-World, Vol. 1. Studies in Phenomenology and Existential Philosophy* (R.M. Zaner and J.T. Engelhardt Jr., Trans.). Evanston, IL: Northwestern University Press. 117, 118, 120

Shah, C. (2012). *Collaborative Information Seeking: The Art and Science of Making the Whole Greater than the Sum of All.* Heidelberg, Germany: Springer Science and Business Media. DOI: 10.1007/978-3-642-28813-5. 90

Shah, C. (2017). *Social Information Seeking: Leveraging the Qisdom of the Crowd.* Cham, Switzerland: Springer. DOI: 10.1007/978-3-319-56756-3. 51, 90

Simon, H. A. (1956). Rational choice and the structure of the environment. *Psychological Review.* 63(2), 129–138. DOI: 10.1037/h0042769. 61

Simon, H. A. (1981). *The Sciences of the Artificial.* Boston: MIT Press. 98

Singer, G., Norbisrath, U., and Lewandowski, D. (2012). Ordinary search engine users assessing difficulty, effort, and outcome for simple and complex search tasks. In *Proceedings of the 4th Information Interaction in Context Symposium* (pp. 110–119). ACM. DOI: 10.1145/2362724.2362746. 37, 38, 40, 44, 45, 56, 58

Smyth, B. (2006). Social and personal: communities and collaboration in adaptive web search. In *Proceedings of the 1st International Conference on Information interaction in Context* (pp. 3–5). ACM. DOI: 10.1145/1164820.1164823. 73

Solomon, P. (1999). Information mosaics: Patterns of action that structure. In T.D. Wilson and D.K. Allen (eds.), *Exploring the Contexts of Information Behavior: Proceedings of the International Conference on Research in Information Needs, Seeking and Use in Different Contexts* (Sheffield, UK, Aug. 13–15, 1998) (pp. 150–175). London: Taylor Graham. 5

Sondhi, P., Chandrasekar, R., and Rounthwaite, R. (2010). Using query context models to construct topical search engines. In *Proceedings of the Third Symposium on Information Interaction in Context* (pp. 75–84). ACM. DOI: 10.1145/1840784.1840797. 74

Sonnenwald, D. H. (1999). Evolving perspectives of human information behavior: Contexts, situations, social networks and information horizons. In T.D. Wilson and D.K. Allen (eds.), *Exploring the Contexts of Information Behavior: Proceedings of the International Conference on Research in Information Needs, Seeking and Use in Different Contexts* (Sheffield, UK, Aug. 13–15, 1998) (pp. 176–190). London: Taylor Graham. 10, 12, 13, 14, 19, 25, 26, 27, 28, 78, 98, 121, 123

Sonnenwald, D. H. (2006). Challenges in sharing information effectively: examples from command and control. *Information Research*, 11(4), paper 270. Retrieved from http://InformationR.net/ir/11-4/paper270.html. 14

Spink, A. (1997). Study of interactive feedback during mediated information retrieval. *Journal of the American Society for Information Science*, 48(5), 382–394. DOI: 10.1002/(SICI)1097-4571(199705)48:5<382::AID-ASI2>3.0.CO;2-R. 5

Spool, J., Scanlon, T., Snyder, C., and DeAngelo, T. (1999). *Web Site Usability: A Designer's Guide*. San Francisco: Morgan Kaufmann. 54, 57

Steinerová, J. (2008). Seeking relevance in academic information use. *Information Research*, 13(4), paper 380. Retrieved from http://InformationR.net/ir/13-4/paper380.html. 36, 38, 40, 42, 43, 52, 53, 61, 64, 65, 66, 67, 68, 69, 71

Sun, Y. and Zhang, Y. (2016). Individual differences and online health information source selection. In *Proceedings of the 2016 ACM Conference on Human Information Interaction and Retrieval* (pp. 321–324). ACM. DOI: 10.1145/2854946.2854989. 37, 40, 46, 47, 64, 66

Suorsa, A. and Huotari M. (2014). Knowledge creation in interactive events. A pilot study in the Joy of Reading program. In *Proceedings of ISIC, the Information Behaviour Conference* (Leeds, Sept. 2–5, 2014). Part 1 (paper isic02). Retrieved from http://InformationR.net/ir/19-4/isic/isic02.html. 36, 39, 40, 48, 49, 50, 51, 52, 53, 70, 71

Sutton, S. A. (1994). The role of attorney mental models of law in case relevance determinations: An exploratory analysis. *Journal of the American Society for Information Science*, 45(3), 186. 10

Swanson, E. B. (1987). Information channel disposition and use. *Decision Science*, 18, 131–145. DOI: 10.1111/j.1540-5915.1987.tb01508.x.

Sweeny, K., Melnyk, D., Miller, W., and Shepperd, J. A. (2010). Information avoidance: Who, what, when, and why. *Review of General Psychology*, 14(4), 340–353. DOI: 10.1037/a0021288. 30, 31, 34

Tabak, E. (2014). Jumping between context and users: A difficulty in tracing information practices. *Journal of the Association for Information Science and Technology*, 65(11), 2223–2232. DOI: 10.1002/asi.23116. 48

Tagore, R. (1922). *East and West. In Creative Unity* (pp. 89-108). New York: The Macmillan Company. 86

Tajfel, H. and Turner, J. C. (1979). An integrative theory of intergroup conflict. In W. G. Austin and S. Worchel (Eds.). *The Social Psychology of Intergroup Relations*. Monterey, CA: Brooks-Cole. 62, 84, 85, 86, 88, 102, 113, 120

Talja, S. (1997). Constituting "information" and "user" as research objects: A theory of knowledge formations as an alternative to the information man-theory. In P. Vakkari, R. Savolainen and B. Dervin (eds.), *Information Seeking in Context: Proceedings of an International Conference on Research in Information Needs, Seeking and Use in Different Contexts* (Tampere, Finland, Aug. 14–16, 1996) (pp. 67–80). London: Taylor Graham. 13

Talja, S., Tuominen, K., and Savolainen, R. (2005). "Isms" in information science: Constructivism, collectivism, and constructionism. *Journal of Documentation*, 61(1), 79–101. DOI: 10.1108/00220410510578023. 5, 15

Taylor, R. S. (1968). Question-negotiation and information seeking in libraries. *College and Research Libraries*, 29(3), 178–194. DOI: 10.5860/crl_29_03_178. 3, 58, 59, 60, 61, 65

Taylor, R. S. (1991). Information use environments. In Dervin, B. and Voigt, M. J. (Eds.), *Progress in Communication Sciences*, 10 (pp. 217–255), Norwood, NJ: Ablex. 4, 9, 55

Tesluk, P. E. and Jacobs, R. R. (1998). Toward an integrated model of work experience. *Personnel Psychology*, 51, 321–355. DOI: 10.1111/j.1744-6570.1998.tb00728.x. 64, 66

Tran, T. A., Schwarz, S., Niederée, C., Maus, H., and Kanhabua, N. (2016). The forgotten needle in my collections: Task-aware ranking of documents in semantic information space. In *Proceedings of the 2016 ACM Conference on Human Information Interaction and Retrieval* (pp. 13–22). ACM. DOI: 10.1145/2854946.2854971. 74

Traxler, J. (2011). Context in a wider context. *MedienPädagogik: Zeitschrift für Theorie und Praxis der Medienbildung*, 19, 1–16. 6, 7, 16, 17, 78

Traxler, J. and Kukulska-Hulme, A. (Eds.). (2016). *Mobile Learning: The Next Generation*. Routledge. 7, 134

Trochim, W. M. (2006). Variables. In *The Research Methods Knowledge Base*, 2nd ed. Retrieved from https://www.socialresearchmethods.net/kb/variable.php. 25, 109

Tuominen, K. and Savolainen, R. (1997). A social constructionist approach to the study of information use as discursive action. In P. Vakkari, R. Savolainen, and B. Dervin (Eds.). *Information Seeking in Context. Proceedings of an International Conference on Research in Information Needs, Seeking and Use in Different Contexts*, Aug. 14–16, 1996, Tampere, Finland. (pp. 81–96). London: Taylor Graham. 15

Vakkari, P. (1999). Task complexity, information types, search strategies and relevance: Integrating studies on information seeking and retrieval. In *Exploring the Contexts of Information Behaviour* (pp. 35–85). London: Taylor Graham. 53

Vakkari, P. (1999). Task complexity, problem structure and information actions: Integrating studies on information seeking and retrieval. *Information Processing and Management*, 35, 819–837. DOI: 10.1016/S0306-4573(99)00028-X. 5

Vakkari, P. (2016). Searching as learning: A systematization based on literature. *Journal of Information Science*, 42(1), 7–18. DOI: 10.1177/0165551515615833. 4

Vancouver, J. B. and Morrison, E. W. (1995). Feedback inquiry: The effect of source attributes and individual difference. *Organizational Behavior and Human Decision Process*, 62, 276–285. DOI: 10.1006/obhd.1995.1050. 71

VandeWalle, D., Genesan, S., Challagalla, G. N., and Bron, S. P. (2000). An integrated model of feedback-seeking behavior: Disposition, context, and cognition. *Journal of Applied Psychology*, 85, 996–1003. DOI: 10.1037/0021-9010.85.6.996. 64, 66

Walsh, G. (1967). Introduction. In A. Schütz. *Phenomenology of the Social World. Studies in Phenomenology and Existential Philosophy* (G. Walsh and F. Lehnert, Trans.). Evanston, IL: Northwestern University Press. 92, 117, 118, 119, 130

Wang, P., Hawk, W. B., and Tenopir, C. (2000). Users' interaction with World Wide Web resources: An exploratory study using a holistic approach. *Information Processing and Management*, 36, 229–251. DOI: 10.1016/S0306-4573(99)00059-X. 63, 66

Weiser, M. (1999). The computer for the 21st century. *Scientific American*, 265(3), 94–104. DOI: 10.1038/scientificamerican0991-94. 72

Widén, G. and Hansen, P. (2012). Managing collaborative information sharing: bridging research on information culture and collaborative information behaviour. *Information Research*, 17(4), paper 538. Retrieved from http://InformationR.net/ir/17-4/paper538.html. 51

Wildemuth, B. M., Freund, L., and Toms, E. G. (2014). Untangling search task complexity and difficulty in the context of interactive information retrieval studies. *Journal of Documentation*, 70(6), 1118–1140. DOI: 10.1108/JD-03-2014-0056. 56, 58

Williamson, K. (1998). Discovered by chance: The role of incidental information acquisition in an ecological model of information use. *Library and Information Science Research*, 20, 23–40. DOI: 10.1016/S0740-8188(98)90004-4. 121

Wilson, P. (1995). Unused relevant information in research and development. *Journal of the American Society for Information Science*, 46, 45–51. DOI: 10.1002/(SICI)1097-4571(199501)46:1<45::AID-ASI5>3.0.CO;2-X. 5

Wilson, T. D. (1997). Information behaviour: An inter-disciplinary perspective. In P. Vakkari, R. Savolainen and B. Dervin (Eds.), *Information Seeking in Context: Proceedings of an Inter-*

national Conference on Research in Information Needs, Seeking and Use in Different Contexts (Tampere, Finland, Aug. 14–16, 1996) (pp. 39–50). London, UK: Taylor Graham. 6

Wilson, T. D. and Walsh, C. (1996). Information behaviour: an interdisciplinary perspective. Sheffield, UK: University of Sheffield, Department of Information Studies. Retrieved from http://informationr.net/tdw/publ/infbehav/index.html. 22, 29, 34, 53

Wilson, T. D. (1981). On user studies and information needs. *Journal of Documentation*, 37, 3–15. DOI: 10.1108/eb026702. 3, 5, 59, 121

Wilson, T. D. (1999). Models in information behaviour research. *Journal of Documentation*, 55(3), 249–270. DOI: 10.1108/EUM0000000007145. 3, 11, 42, 43

Wilson, T. D. (2000). Human information behaviour. *Informing Science*, 3(2), 49–55. DOI: 10.28945/576. 4

Wilson, T. D. (2010). Information sharing: an exploration of the literature and some propositions. *Information Research*, 15(4), paper 440. Retrieved from http://InformationR.net/ir/15-4/paper440.html. 47

Wu, T. F., Custer, R. L., and Dyrenfurth, M. J. (1996). Technology and personal problem solving styles. *Journal of Technology Education*, 7(2), 55–71. 63, 66

Xu, Y. and Chen, Z. (2006). Relevance judgment: What do information users consider beyond topicality? *Journal of the American Society for Information Science and Technology*, 57(7), 961–973. DOI: 10.1002/asi.20361. 67, 69

Xu, Y. (C.), Tan, C.Y. (B.) and Yang, L. (2006). Who Will You Ask? An Empirical Study of Interpersonal Task Information Seeking. *Journal of the American Society for Information Science and Technology*, 57(12), 1666–1677. DOI: 10.1002/asi.20339. 46, 56, 58, 59, 61, 64, 66, 67, 69

Yates, C. and Partridge, H. (2015). Citizens and social media in times of natural disaster: exploring information experience. *Information Research*, 20(1), paper-659. 10

Yitzhaki, M. and Hammershlag, G. (2004). Accessibility and use of information sources among computer scientists and software engineers in Israel: Academy versus industry. *Journal of the American Society for Information Science and Technology*, 55(9), 832–842. DOI: 10.1002/asi.20026. 59, 61

Zhang, L., Kopak, R., Freund, L., and Rasmussen, E. (2011). Making functional units functional: The role of rhetorical structure in use of scholarly journal articles. *International Journal of Information Management*, 31(1), 21–29. DOI: 10.1016/j.ijinfomgt.2010.10.003. 4

Zimmermann, A., Lorenz, A., and Oppermann, R. (2007). An operational definition of context. In B. Kokinov, D.C. Richardson, T.R. Roth-Berghofer, and L. Vieu (Eds.) *Proceedings of the 6th International and Interdisciplinary Conference on Modeling and Using Context, CONTEXT 2007* (Roskilde, Denmark, Aug. 20–24). Lecture Notes in Computer Science, 4635 (pp. 558–571), Berlin, Germany: Springer. DOI: 10.1007/978-3-540-74255-5_42. 78, 134

Author's Biography

Naresh Agarwal is an Associate Professor at the Simmons School of Library and Information Science (College of Organizational, Computational, and Information Sciences) in Boston, Massachusetts. He earned his Ph.D. from the National University of Singapore (NUS)'s Department of Information Systems, School of Computing. Naresh has published more than 40 articles in international journals, conference proceedings, and as book chapters in the fields of information behavior and knowledge management. As of November 2017, researchers have cited his work more than 370 times (as listed by Google Scholar). Naresh looks at the way people look for information and the contextual factors that impact their choice of information sources. He seeks to understand and synthesize the apparent contradictions in this phenomenon and tries to reconcile multiple perspectives. Apart from seeking, Naresh also studies serendipitous information encountering and the causes and effects—both on the recipient and the sender—of information stopping and information avoidance behaviors, especially by people who use smartphones and social media. Naresh teaches courses in technology and web development, theories of information science, knowledge management, and evaluation of information services. He has held various leadership positions at ASIS&T (the Association for Information Science and Technology). He was a member of its Board of Directors from 2012–2014. Naresh was the Chair of its Membership Committee (2015–2017), the Conference Co-Chair of its 80th Annual Meeting, Washington, D.C., Oct. 27–Nov. 1, 2017, and he was awarded the ASIS&T James M. Cretsos Leadership Award in 2012. Prior to entering the doctoral program at NUS, Naresh worked for six years in technology roles in the voice-over-IP, bioInformatics, and digital cinema industries. You can learn more about him at http://web.simmons.edu/~agarwal.